happiness is homemaking

By

ELLA MAY MILLER

MOODY PRESS

CHICAGO

© 1974 by
THE MOODY BIBLE INSTITUTE
OF CHICAGO

ISBN: 0-8024-3410-X

Printed in the United States of America

CONTENTS

PREFACE

IT IS POPULAR for the modern woman to resent being a housewife, to feel it is a second-rate profession. This need not be the case.

Homemaking can be enjoyable, when you join hands with God.

I believe it is the most important and rewarding career for the woman to choose to be a wife and mother. She will have interests outside the home, to be sure, but they should be secondary.

This book is a compilation of some of my radio talks on "Heart to Heart"— the program bringing inspiration to the homemaker in the midst of her everyday tasks. Included in these talks are excerpts from actual letters from homemakers who listen to the program.

I hope you will like this heart-to-heart volume. Happy homemaking!

1

PLANT HAPPINESS

PLANT HAPPINESS

First plant five rows of peas: Prayer, Perseverance, Politeness, Promptness, Purity.

Next plant three rows of squash: Squash gossip, Squash criticism, and Squash indifference.

Then five rows of lettuce: Let us be faithful to duty. Let us be unselfish. Let us be truthful. Let us follow Christ. Let us love another.

No garden is complete without turnips: Turn up for church. Turn up with a smile. Turn up with new ideas. Turn up with determination to make everything count for something good and worthwhile.

AUTHOR UNKNOWN

Have you ever seen a homemaker who is desperately trying to find happiness? She probably finds herself more miserable at the end of the day. She fails to realize that happiness is in the heart, that little things—like clean curtains, a flower, a baby's smile—bring happiness.

Someone has said that you should do something every day to make someone else happy, even if it's just leaving them alone! Another observation is that some people bring happiness wherever they go, others whenever they go!

Seriously though, happiness is a by-product of our thinking, acting, and living.

KINDNESS

"The secret of true happiness is to do a little kindness to someone every day."

Every day you can, and should be, planting seeds of happiness in your life as well as in your husband's life, in the life of each child, and in the life of everyone you contact.

One of these seeds is kindness. Happiness comes from the knowledge that you are of some use in the world. The philosophy of happiness is expressed in the old Hindu proverb, "Help thy brother's boat across and, lo! Thine own has reached the shore."

A young wife asked her husband what he would like to bring home for supper. He was startled to hear her interested note, then answered, "A bag of white beans."

She exclaimed, "Beans! Isn't there something else?"

"No," he insisted, "just fix these for me tonight." She carried out his wishes. That evening at the table he remarked, "Thanks, honey, for fixing these beans. Supper was delicious tonight."

As she related this incident to me, the wife laughed, "I thought that was the most foolish request I had ever heard. White beans! But I decided if that was what he liked I'd fix them." She added, "Previously we had been having spats and quarrels, but that evening was different. We were all happy."

When you lay aside the ironing to play with your child or to take a walk in the woods, you are not only making his day happy, you are contributing to his future life. If you make your child happy now, you will make him happy twenty years from now by the memory of it.

SOMEONE TO LOVE

Happiness comes in having someone to love. You can be happy as you meet the challenges presented by

8

your family. And it is in loving, not in being loved, that you are blessed.

Today you can show your love in a special way to your husband, to each child. Let them know they are wanted and appreciated. Establish harmonious relationships with your children, based on your love and harmony as parents, and based on attitudes of good will, tolerance, and understanding. Love goes beyond mere duty.

HAPPINESS FROM WITHIN

Happiness comes from within. "Whenever you see a woman seeking happiness outside of herself, you can be sure she has never yet found it," says F. Lincicome.

Let me warn you right now, your search is futile if you have been hunting happiness in your clubs, bridge parties, bowling scores, or if you have been hunting happiness in fame, wealth, or possessions.

You are not happy because you have something. You are happy with what you have, or with what you do not have.

A Greek philosopher promised his king that he would be happy as soon as he found a happy man and put on his shirt. It so happened that when the king found the happy man, the man had no shirt.

IN YOUR THOUGHTS

Your happiness comes from the character of your thoughts and attitudes about the tasks and situations you find right at home and about the daily routine ones, as well as the more pleasurable ones. Keep in mind each loved one and how the daily tasks help to accomplish your goals for them.

Happiness has no reason and cannot be found in the facts of your life. It does come in the color of the light by which you look at the facts.

Happiness does not depend upon a full pocketbook or a full schedule, but upon a mind full of rich thoughts and a heart full of rich emotions.

Abraham Lincoln said, "Folks are generally as happy as they make up their minds to be."

In Your Hands

"Happiness is in your hands" says the educator and sculptor Boris Blai. He believes that a major source of today's neurosis, the *why* of so many jittery worried people, is simply that we are using "our heads too much and our hands too little." God has given us our hands to use. When they become idle and clumsy, we are trying to buck nature.

Maybe modern laborsaving devices for homemakers have done us more damage than good! Maybe Grandma's seemingly endless, tiresome, and constant labors kept her happy. At least we sometimes imagine that she was happier than the average twentieth century housewife.

Did Grandma's secret of happiness lie in her ability to be manually occupied and to see the finished product, that which *she* had accomplished? Probably her enthusiasm in her work helped. Happiness does not come from easy work, but from the afterglow of satisfaction following the achievement of a difficult task that demanded your best. It comes not from doing what you like, but from liking what you do.

Charles Kingsley said, "We act as if comfort and luxury were the chief requirements of life, when all that we need to make us really happy is something to be enthusiastic about." This is in sharp contrast to today's philosophy which implies you will find happiness apart from your responsibilities.

Here are three simple rules for happiness: something to do, someone to love, something to hope for.

To me, the last rule—something to hope for—is the most significant of the three. Without hope, something to do and someone to love can be cold. The Bible says: "Blessed (happy) is the man . . . whose hope the Lord is" (Jeremiah 17:7).

Real happiness comes in forgetting self. You forget self as you get interested in Jesus Christ. As you fix your eyes, your goals, and your mind on Him, then you see beyond daily incidents. You see beyond sorrow, pain, loss, and heartaches. You see Him! He also helps you to see others and to find something to do for them. If there is no one on this earth you have as your own to love—you have Him.

You are not out seeking joy. No, joy comes to you as a fruit, a natural product of just being a branch on the True Vine. "The fruit of the Spirit is . . . joy" (Galatians 5:22).

That is not all. The Bible says: "If in this life only we have hope in Christ, we are of all men most miserable" (1 Corinthians 15:19).

What is this hope beyond present life that brings joy? It is the hope of final perfection, of complete salvation in Jesus Christ—salvation from all sin and evil, from all sorrow, pain, and disappointments, and from all unkindness, tension, and frustration. Salvation will be complete as we join Christ in the endless years.

This hope brings joy?

Let us explain it this way. Your child is away from home. He overcomes much of his loneliness and disappointment as he thinks about the day when he will be home with you. This hope helps keep him happy. In a similar way, the hope in a future with Christ brings happiness to anyone! It keeps us centered on Him.

11

Happiness can be yours now, right at home! In whatever circumstance you may find yourself, you *can* experience true happiness in Christ.

2

BE A CREATIVE HOMEMAKER

Do YOU FEEL that life has given you a raw deal? Has every other woman's life, home, and family seemed more interesting than yours?

I am reminded of the words of Dr. John A. Schindler, "A woman's life is only drab if she is drab." He further states that a woman who has the curiosity and desire can know more of the world about her, especially that part in which she is an expert—the human relations part. With imagination and talents, with the capacity and control of herself, she can create and bring about those ideas she visualizes. This is creative life!

"Creativity," someone has said, "is nothing more than applied imagination." It should not be confused with intelligence, experience, or skill. Many men, women, and children with average intellectual accomplishments possess a strong creative faculty. The ones who are born with it are at a tremendous advantage. The rest of us can, at least in part, acquire it. We homemakers do need this "applied imagination" in every area of home and family living. It helps make living satisfying and enjoyable.

IN HUSBAND-WIFE RELATIONSHIPS

Someone else stated: "There is satisfying, creative identity for the woman who feels that she is the one most responsible for shaping the kind of person her child is to become—the most responsible for the well-being of her husband; the most responsible for making her family life good."

Your greatest task as homemaker is to create companionship between you and your husband. When you accomplish this, creativity in your housework and in your relationships with the children will be much easier.

Create a cheerful, pleasant environment for husband to come home to. Naturally, it will have to be within certain limits: the kind of house you live in, your means and ability, his interests and likes.

Be creative in encouraging him in his work and his hobbies. I do not mean creative like one wife was, who bought her husband a $100 set of golf clubs for his birthday. Really, she did not buy it. She charged it to his account. However, he cannot play golf, nor does he even care to learn how! (On second thought, she *was* creative! In a negative way—creating trouble and hard feelings!)

CREATIVE HOUSEKEEPING

A homemaker can be creative in cooking and baking. Try new dishes, but not necessarily exotic or expensive ones. If you have been used to ready-prepared foods, try preparing some foods from a recipe, especially baked foods. You will have lots of fun and satisfaction.

IRONING IS CREATIVE

Even ironing is creative—if you think so.

Joyce confessed, "I used to be lazy—just watch TV or talk to the neighbors. I'd let the children run around with wrinkled and soiled clothes. My husband pulled his shirts out of the basket to wear to work. I didn't know how to iron, and I didn't want to learn." This surprised me, for she irons beautifully, even takes in

14

ironing to supplement her husband's meager wages. She continued, "I decided one day to see how nicely I could iron their clothes. Now I think it's fun!"

Joyce is a creative homemaker, making something attractive and nice out of jobs she *has* to do!

CREATIVITY IS ACQUIRED

I, for one, am grateful that creativity can be acquired. I have always wished I were more creative, like one of my friends whose lovely slip covers I admire. She covered the sofa and two chairs one night after her family had gone to sleep.

As I ohed and ahed, this friend's daughter complimented her mother, "Oh, that's just like Mama. She always could make something pretty out of nothing."

I was also amazed recently at our daughter-in-law's creative ability. Instead of sewing her little girl's dresses exactly as the pattern, she adds a flower appliqué, an attractive rickrack border, or a fancy stitch. On one little red sunsuit was an appliqué of a sailboat. She has beautified their small apartment with attractive curtains made from denim.

CHILDREN LEARN TO BE CREATIVE

Probably the most creative act for parents is helping to bring a new life into existence, caring for it, and shaping its character and life. And a mother needs to continue creativity in her relationships with her children, thereby teaching them how to be creative. Parents should not buy everything ready-made for them. We should place raw materials in their hands with which they can use their imagination. According to their ages and abilities, they should have blocks, crayons, paper, blunt scissors, Tinkertoys, or other toy-building materials.

15

Girls love to help bake pies or cookies, make paper dolls, and sew for real dolls. The older girl can help redo her bedroom. She can paint, make a vanity dresser from orange crates, and sew curtains. Sewing, cooking, and baking, as well as music and art, are creative outlets for her.

Both boys and girls can help fix up around the house. They can do a good job with flower beds, or a garden if you have space for one.

Boys love to build bird houses, dog houses, or tree houses. Given a book of instructions, they enjoy making carts, kites, boats, or simple pieces of furniture.

FRANKIE

One mother tells how her boys had worked many weeks to build a fort in the nearby woods. One day their city cousin Frankie arrived, and off they rushed to see the wonderful accomplishment. In a few moments a group of dejected boys returned. When the mother inquired what happened, they replied, "Frankie laughed at it!"

Upon hearing this, Frankie's mother quickly replied, "Now, boys, don't let it bother you. I'm sure that you have a lovely fort, but to him it has to come out of a mail-order catalog to be something nice."

I feel sorry for Frankie, but it is hardly his fault. Evidently he was taught to expect everything ready-made.

This also carries over to children's entertainment. Do not give it to them canned. Teach them games, verses, and songs. Encourage them to participate in healthy sports, in service activities, and to take an active part in church programs.

CREATING CHARACTER IN CRISIS

One mother says she receives great satisfaction in creating character in crisis. That is a challenge! In spite of horrid comics, pornography, sensual advertising, and shows, she is grateful for the many good books available from religious publishers, as well as those in the public libraries. She helps her children choose the good literature and programs.

In an age of riots and protests, she is teaching her children to participate in positive church and community activities. These help others and build bridges of love between clashing groups. She believes parents must give of their time and energy to help create character in a time of crisis. Although wars rage, and pornography and sensualism send out their stench, parents can still find God and good if they search for Him and His way of creative living.

CREATE FAMILY TRADITIONS

Another mother had spent most of her childhood in a home for children from broken homes. Although she was treated well, she realized how much she missed by not having her own family—a father, mother, brothers, sisters—people to love because they were her own.

So now she is eager to create interesting family traditions for her children. One time a birthday cake was lopsided, so she anchored it with a toothpick. When one little fellow found it, he complained because his piece had an "ole toothpick in it."

Immediately this mother responded, "It does? That means you're the lucky one who gets the kiss." She got up and planted a kiss in the middle of his forehead.

From that day on there has been a toothpick in every cake. Even the teenager still claims his kiss when he is the lucky one.

You may not be creative in precisely this way. However, realizing your importance as homemaker and feeling that you are responsible to make family life good helps you acquire an extra creative touch. Perhaps it is just a flower on the table, or bread or cookies that are homemade instead of store-bought, or a smile when things go wrong! You know what is in your imagination; just apply it to everyday living. That is creative living!

LIFE NOT DRAB

So, homemaker, do not give up in despair. Take a moment to relax. Enumerate the abilities and talents God has given to you. Then ask Him to show you how you can use them in creating a happier, more interesting home for your husband and for each child.

Life is only drab if you make it that way!

3

FIND YOUR IDENTITY

THE SEARCH FOR IDENTITY begins early. We are restless until we discover who we are, where we are going and why, what the meaning and purpose is in life, and how we belong.

This is the search of the hippie, the yippie, the protester, the delinquent, the alcoholic, or any other individual who reacts strongly to himself and to society.

SALLY

Sally came to me with tears in her eyes. It was fully five minutes before she could control her voice. And then she began to talk—in short sentences, with long pauses between each one.

After listening many minutes, I summed up Sally's problem. She cannot accept herself. She is not too interested in working toward a career.

Sally needs to recognize that she can never be anyone but Sally. She can never be like her efficient, capable, outgoing sister. Nor as a single person can she live in her dream world of becoming a wife and mother. She desperately needs to accept herself just as she is, and define worthy goals for herself now, as a single girl. Should her Romeo come along, then she could realize her dream.

Sally happens to be a single girl in search of her identity. But many married women join her in this search.

And the currently popular argument that only professional work enables a woman to find herself is not the answer. Neither is the complete answer in bathing babies and baking bread.

The basic questions are not if a woman should work, stay at home, do volunteer work, or go to school. These are important decisions, but for each women the answers depend on her reply to the more fundamental questions of Who am I? What are my true values? What do I want to accomplish?

Although many women claim that marriage and motherhood hinder them from finding themselves, basically a girl's desire is to be married and to be a mother. Her body and her emotions are created for giving and receiving love, concern, compassion, and tenderness—becoming one with someone of the opposite sex. God designed her this way.

Again, I come back to emphasize—the one who has already chosen wifehood and motherhood must give priority to adapting her life to meet her husband's and children's needs. When she has met these needs, then she can work toward other goals which do not conflict with her primary responsibility.

UNPREPARED

Jane, a housewife from New Jersey, admits that frustration kept her from finding her identity. She was totally unprepared to cope with her family, with her big house, with superfluity of possessions, and with the taxi service required of a suburban mother. This unpreparedness in the skills of wifehood, motherhood, and housekeeping made her tense and frustrated. Added to this was the feeling she was wasting her education.

Only when she began doing her work for the Lord did she begin to enjoy her homemaking career.

Jane concludes, "I can think of no greater satisfaction than to be a housewife. There is nothing that can give you more pride than a good, Christian husband and fine, intelligent, interesting children who also think seriously of their Christian obligations. Also there's no greater happiness than the creativity of setting a beautiful table, decorating a birthday cake, preparing a good meal, decorating a room attractively, and making the windows and furniture shine!"

MODERN PRESSURES

The pressure of being unprepared is a large factor in hindering the modern homemaker from finding herself.

There is also the pressure of authority. Do not misunderstand me. I am not referring to an authoritative setup for society, but rather, the authority of the specialists. There are "authorities" on everything—on marriage relations, on child-rearing, on housekeeping. Adding to this pressure is the disagreement among the authorities. This often puts the homemaker in a worse plight than before reading their articles. She is afraid to do what she believes she should do.

Another alarming factor is women's gullibility to high-pressure salesmanship. Television, radio, magazines, manufacturers, newspapers, and catalogues offer her a choice daily. So she buys brands, or switches from one to another, in an attempt to have the happiest family on her block.

Social mobility is another contribution to the modern world's dilemma. She moves from one community to another. In each location, customs differ from where she grew up. Wanting to be accepted, she tries to conform. A housewife who grew up in Los Angeles says she learned to serve the salad first. In Ohio it should be served with the steak. But in New York it is served afterwards!

KNOW YOURSELF

Such pressures create confusion and bewilderment for the modern homemaker. She cannot be her honest self. This affects her attitudes and relationships. She feels restricted in the home and decides to ignore family obligations because she feels she can only find herself outside the home.

Norman W. Paget, Executive Director of the Family Service Agency of San Bernardino, California, says it is rare that a woman with such an attitude becomes successful. He advises her to "narrow her field," and not to allow "cheap outside pressures" to persuade her. Her family should know where her interests lie. He believes, "The woman who tries to be all things to all people and nothing to herself is betraying her intelligence, her sex, and the very humanity which she is supposed to be particularly able to defend."[1]

So homemaker, be honest with yourself. Define your goals, your values in life. Know your abilities. And accept where God has placed you. Ask Him to help you become your true self.

HONESTY

Many a homemaker, all excited about being honest with herself, misinterprets it, as was the case with Cora. She made the decision to become a person, to be an individual. So she stayed in bed as late as she wanted to. She prepared meals only when she felt like it. She did the laundry just when she had an urge. The children

1. *Why Young Mothers Feel Trapped,* ed. Robert Stein (New York: Trident, 1965), p. 18.

often wore dirty clothes. Her husband frequently ironed his own shirt before going to work. You see, she had to be honest with herself.

Cora followed this pattern of honesty in all of her homemaking responsibilities, but still was dissatisfied. So she decided to go back to college. But in so doing, she has almost completely isolated herself from her family.

Cora stubbornly insists, "I must be myself."

However, in moments of true honesty, she confides her disappointment, increased dissatisfaction, frustrations, and tensions.

Honesty does *not* mean, as currently interpreted, that you say whatever comes to your mind and do just as you pretty please. Far from it!

Honesty does *not* mean following every impulse, passion, or selfish whim.

However, honesty does mean finding out who you are—your likes and dislikes, your strengths and weaknesses. Honesty is evaluating your goals and purposes in life.

Honesty is facing reality—the kind of husband, children, house, neighborhood you have. Honesty is accepting them, working together with them and within the framework of the culture and community you live in.

GLAD TO BE A WOMAN

I believe that no woman who has chosen marriage and motherhood can find her identity outside her home, when such a search keeps her from establishing warm, loving, satisfying relationships.

Psychiatrist Marie N. Robinson states that the woman who finds herself is very glad to be a woman, with all the responsibilities, joys, and duties which are uniquely hers. Down deep inside, she feels profoundly secure and safe with herself and her husband. She delights in giving to

23

those she loves. Psychiatrists calls this the "essential feminine altruism." She does not resent but enjoys giving her best to her husband and children.

Mrs. Robinson concludes, "When a woman does not have this instinctively based altruism available to her, or when she denies that it is a desirable trait, life's continuous small misfortunes leave her in a glowering rage, helpless and beside herself with self-pity."[2]

FIND GOD'S PLAN

I would add further that the woman finds her identity because in all honesty, with herself and her Creator, she has *found* and *accepted* God's will for her.

Her purpose for existing is to glorify God. She accomplishes this as she faithfully and lovingly gives herself first to her family, and then to those around her.

2. *The Power of Sexual Surrender* (New York: Signet, 1959), p. 32.

4

DISCIPLINE YOUR LIFE

Are some persons just lucky?
Or born under the right star?
Or do they have a part
In becoming what they are?

AUTHOR UNKNOWN

THE RESPONSE, according to Frank Curtis Williams, is:
"Man is still responsible . . . His success lies not with
the stars but with himself. He must carry on the fight
of self-correction and discipline."

Translate this into a homemaker's world: it says,
"You will never be the homemaker you can be if you
do just what you feel like doing. Pressure, tension, and
discipline are a part of life."

DEFINITION

I think it is unfortunate that when we hear the word
discipline, we usually think of punishment.

Actually the dictionary defines discipline as "training
of the mind or character," or a "trained condition of
order and obedience." The concept of "punish" is at the
end of the long list of definitions.[1]

To arrive at "order and obedience," there needs to be
correction, sometimes punishment. That is one method
of learning—not only for children, but also for adults.

1. *Thorndike-Barnhart Comprehensive Desk Dictionary*, 1955 ed.,
s.v. "discipline."

25

I believe the center of life is our thoughts. Here then is the starting point for discipline. Thoughts then become words and actions. That is why it is so essential to discipline thoughts.

Disciplining thoughts takes real effort, but it is possible. It is a choice we make.

I choose to focus either on the positive or on the negative. I choose to think about the weaknesses and mistakes, or to think good, kind thoughts about my husband and child, about my neighbors and friends. I can choose to focus on their strengths, on what I appreciate and like about them, and plan kind, thoughtful deeds and surprises.

I can focus my thoughts on the tasks and responsibilities of the day and how to get them done happily and creatively, or I can grumble and complain about them.

The Bible reminds us to have the thoughts of Christ— to think on all that is true, honest, just, pure, lovely, of good report, virtuous, and praise.

No one else can do this for you. God will help you discipline your thoughts, but you choose what you think about most of the day.

DEFINE GOALS

Some homemakers never really know what they want out of life. They never clearly define their goals or objectives. They settle for whatever comes. But are never satisfied or happy.

Dorothy discovered this early in her marriage. Her husband's job began at eight o'clock, so she began sleeping in. Soon she realized that something had happened to their relationship. They were not open and honest with each other. She sensed a distance but did not know why. Dorothy began sincerely searching her own mind and their experiences. The only change she could discover in their lives together was her sleeping in.

Without saying a word to her husband, she began getting up and fixing the food. They breakfasted together. Within several days they were again communicating honestly and freely.

Then she questioned her husband. He admitted that although he had told her to sleep in, he did not enjoy eating breakfast alone. Beginning the day together made his entire day better.

Dorothy said, "I had to discipline myself. It wasn't easy, because I kept rationalizing, 'Why can't I sleep those extra twenty minutes?' But when I remembered what it meant to my husband and to our relationship, that was reward enough. Besides, I don't even miss those few minutes of sleep," she laughed, "and I do get extra things done getting up earlier. Or some mornings I lie down after he's gone and relax for a few moments."

Your husband may prefer to eat alone. But you know what requires discipline in your life to reach your objective of happy relationships. It takes a lot out of you. You have to give up some desires that stand in the way of reaching your goal. It is worth it, though! Try it. You will discover the truth of this statement.

EVERY AREA

We all need to work at disciplines in every area—our time, money, energy, emotions, and wants.

I know a homemaker whose husband gave her the choice of a new stove or an automatic washer. She needed the stove badly. But she chose the washer, thinking, "I'll get the washer, and when he sees me struggling with preparing meals on the hot plate he'll soon get me the stove. I'll get both of them."

But that did not happen. She was stuck with the hot

plate for many months because she did not discipline her wants.

When I go shopping, I have to really discipline myself. It is so easy to purchase things I really do not have money for or need.

ORDER AND CONTROLS

A contented life, a good day, is impossible without order and controls.

Many homemakers spend hours on the phone, before the TV, calling on friends, or reading; then they are frustrated because the housework is not done.

A letter came recently from a woman who said her home and marriage almost fell apart because she would just sleep most of the morning. There was so much to do she hated to get started!

Another homemaker's marriage did end because she just did not keep up with daily routine. Meals were seldom ready. Her husband would come home after a hard day's work, and she wouldn't even have supper planned, let alone ready to serve. His shirts were never ironed. Most of the time he could not find clean clothes.

It is possible to make each day a good day. Praise the Lord! It takes determination, willpower, and guidelines as well as the knowledge that you are appreciated as a homemaker.

A DAILY SCHEDULE

Mary's husband commended her on the good work she was doing. This pleased her so that she set up a daily schedule to include meal preparation, cleaning kitchen, making beds, and playing with the children.

On regular days she does the laundry and ironing. She includes time for the family, too. But Mary is flexible within her schedule, alert to family needs which take priority.

We need controls in our personal lives, too. Our daily schedule should provide for a period of quiet time—relaxation and rest. It could include reading and meditating, Bible study, prayer, a short nap.

We should plan some social activities and service projects in the week's schedule. There are always neighbors, friends, or someone in the church group who needs encouragement and help in some way.

DISCIPLINES FOR CHILDREN

A disciplined life for the child includes some daily routines. This can be carried out too strictly, I know. But pity the child who never has known some sort of controls and routine, including regular eating and sleeping habits; carrying through a daily responsibility—like feeding a cat, or helping in the house, or with the chores; finishing the food on his plate; regular Bible reading, prayers, and church attendance; responsibility for his actions; learning the value of money; and learning how to express negative feelings in a creative way.

TAKES DISCIPLINED PARENT

It takes a disciplined parent to discipline children. By discipline, I mean teaching what they need to do today, now, in order to realize the goals you parents have established for happy family living.

For example: Your goal today is a family picnic after Father comes home from work. So you have to get the work done, including picnic preparations. You will help motivate the children when they lag. Oh, you will allow them occasional rest or fun periods, but these will be limited. Your goal controls you, keeps you from taking time out to read that exciting book, and keeps the children from loafing.

Discipline also includes teaching right from wrong, helping the children acquire a set of true values.

Dr. Paul R. Hortin, a Florida minister, asks, "Should we discipline our children?" Then he answers, "Yes, indeed! If parents neglect this Christian duty, then the police will have to do it for them."

AFFECTS ADULT LIFE

A disciplined life in early years affects adult life.

A study in 1959, made by Dr. Dale B. Harris, director of the Institute of Child Welfare at the University of Minnesota, was quite revealing. The institute compared two groups of adults who had gone through nursery school in the 1920s. One group came from homes with strict standards. The parents closely supervised the child's schooling, contacts, and experiences. The second group came from homes where the child had much more liberty to do as he pleased.

The study found that adults who came from the disciplined group had more self-respect and confidence. They were more satisfied with their jobs and family life. They also had happier memories of their childhood.[3]

Love must show through our daily routine and disciplines. The two go hand in hand. One without the other does not help the child establish inner controls.

Even God disciplines the one who loves Him, so he will be a better person.

Is your goal a satisfying and contented life including happy, meaningful relationships with your family? This requires establishing good habits. It includes controls and much self-discipline. God wants to help you reach your goal!

3. *Coronet,* June 1959, p. 8.

5

PRAYER IS POWER

HOMEMAKER, how are things going today? Pretty
smoothly? Or is everything going wrong?

In either case, have you tried prayer?

Now, I am not one who believes that you can use
prayer to manipulate God to satisfy your every whim.
One homemaker prayed each wash day that God would
not let it rain until all the clothes were dry, and when
He did not comply, she would be grumpy until she
finally dried the last sock.

No, I do not believe in such demands to insure a
smooth day without any wrinkles.

But I do feel very keenly the need of Someone to help
me through the day, to give me wisdom and discernment.

That Someone is God. Through prayer I get His wisdom, strength, and power to face the day's experiences.

Prayer is nothing more than talking to God. It may
be verbal when you get into that closet and shut the
door and pour out your heart's desires, problems, failures, successes, and joys. It may not be the closet.
Prayer may be through your thoughts as you go about
those routine tasks which become automatic and leave
your mind free. Or prayer may be the communion of
your spirit with God's Spirit—without words or recog-
nizable thoughts.

The kind of prayer I am thinking about is not free, effortless magic. It is prayer that reaches God, that succeeds. It requires effort and discipline. Such praying includes four elements: adoration, confession, thanksgiving, and supplication.

Now let me explain.

Begin your prayers with *adoration* and praise. Take time out to meditate on who God is and what He has been doing and is doing for you. Praise Him for His beautiful world. Praise Him for whatever happens to you. This turns the situation into a blessing.

Next comes *confession*. Mention those sins that muddy up your mind: those unkind, ugly, critical thoughts about your neighbors, your husband, your child, your parents, your in-laws, the president, or other leaders. Confess those impure thoughts, those selfish words and acts that have hurt God and others. Confess them; yes, ask for forgiveness.

Then begin *thanksgiving*. Pull out at least one thing you can thank Him for. Even if you think there is absolutely nothing good in your life or circumstances, thank Him for breath, for salvation, for sins forgiven, for His promises of peace of mind, and for hope of heaven where there is no more pain, sorrow, or death.

Now the channel between you and God is clean and open. Because He is holy, He demands this cleansed condition from you.

You are ready now to begin *supplication*. Ask and you will receive. Not always in the way you thought you would, because God's thoughts are so much higher and better than yours.

You will receive when you ask according to God's will, when you mean "Thy will be done," and not selfishly to gratify your wants! *Ask*, and you will receive all you need. *Seek*, and you will find His will for you.

Knock, and He will open doors of peace, contentment, joy, and service.

PRAYER IS REAL

Someone has written, "The great mistake made by many Christians with regard to prayer is that they take important matters to God and attempt to manage smaller concerns themselves. This is really unbelief, for it is doubting His interest in us, and forgetting that Word which says, "Without me ye can do nothing."

> O what peace we often forfeit,
> O what needless pain we bear,
> All because we do not carry
> Everything to God in prayer!
> —JOSEPH SCRIVEN

Prayer has become so real to me—as a child separated from home and lonely in difficult school days, as a bride and missionary, and as a mother. I have prayed very specifically for each child—even before birth. I know God has blessed our children in many ways, in answer to prayer.

From the day they were born I thanked God for their normal, healthy bodies. And when they started with fever or pain or headaches, I would always tell God about it, asking for wisdom to know what to do.

If they did not respond to simple home treatments, then we contacted a doctor and continued to pray for God's healing and guidance, and gave thanks.

We have had some serious illnesses and near-death situations. These were laid before God in special prayers, requesting His healing, according to His will.

As a mother concerned for her children in their plans for education, securing jobs, finding a life companion— for all these and many more day-by-day situations and long-range goals, I have prayed. I also pray for relatives, neighbors, friends and for world conditions. And I am convinced that I am alive today because of prayer.

PRAY IN FAITH

God does not make life a bed of roses—not at all! But when you pray, He takes the worries away. You can approach daily living in a positive, creative, contented way using your energy and powers constructively—to change or control the difficult situations, or to be able to accept what He allows to remain.

If you ask, believing—He answers. If you ask that He receive the glory, then you can accept *how* He answers.

We, too often, have our own ideas and wishes. And, when we pray, we expect God to answer according to our wishes in the way we have decided. When He answers differently than we expect, we fail to recognize it. We become discouraged or critical and wonder why He does not answer. It is not wrong to think things through. To have your own ideas is OK, but when we pray, we must be ready to accept God's way.

There is no excuse not to pray.

Pray when you are waiting for the red light to turn green. One young housewife walks several blocks to catch the bus to work. At the first street she prays for her husband, at the next street for her in-laws, at the third corner for her minister, and so on till she reaches the bus stop. Every day she enjoys a prayer walk.

Especially in times like these we mothers need to pray for our children instead of worrying about them. We want the best for our children in preparing them to face life maturely, to make wise decisions. But we often become overanxious.

PRAYER IS POWER

Prayer not only helps solve parenthood problems,

34

it also transforms a woman's personal life, gives her that beauty of inner strength and character.

Someone has said, "In true prayer we do get away from the earth awhile, we come near to the thought of God, and get what might be called 'a God's eye view of the world.' We measure all life's striving with a truer, divine perspective. We see the things in life that matter most. Then we come back to our problems and duties with a true sense of values."

A moment with God in prayer helps me get rid of wrong attitudes, wrong feelings and emotions. It gives me new insights and understanding.

I believe that our nation can only come through today's crisis successfully if we pray not just formal prayers at worship services, but in intercessory prayers in prayer groups, in our closets, behind closed doors, and about our work. Prayer is far more than saying words. As the hymn says, "Prayer is the heart's sincere desire, unuttered or expressed." And I believe we women must carry this prayer burden if we want God to act. We must pray daily!

I Need God

God promises, "If ye abide in me, and my words abide in you, ye shall ask what ye will, and it shall be done unto you" (John 15:7).

God never changes His spoken word. When we maintain a close, intimate relationship with Him of love and obedience, then He hears and answers.

Prayer simply acknowledges that I do depend on God, that there are some needs I cannot meet, some demands I am unable to fulfill with my own wisdom or resources. That is what prayer says—I need God.

Just as a child needs to share his thoughts, his wishes, and his wants with his earthly parent, I, in the same way, need to talk things over with God.

35

Prayer is power.

We must take the time, effort, and energy to pray. Then God takes over. But until we do that, He stands by helpless, simply because we do not allow Him to work.

Because God is who He is, prayer is power.

6

THE FREEDOM OF MARRIAGE

A NEW YORK PSYCHOLOGIST, Dr. Harold Greenwald, advocates common-law marriage—a nonlegal, voluntary association.

His reasoning is that people would stay together because they wanted to, not because they are obligated to. In other words, if there is no law, then you are not guilty of breaking it.

Actually, to nonlegalize marriage would take away any decent approach to family life. In our deep concern about juvenile delinquency, I am surprised and perturbed that these sociologists and psychologists are advocating doing away with legal marriage.

GOD'S WAY

Regardless of being popular with many, this approach does not rate in God's Book. Marriage—legal and responsible marriage—is already established by Him. His marriage law was passed ages ago, regardless of whether or not modern man decides to ignore it. I, for one, believe that His way is the best way—for any culture, in any age!

A society without moral laws, without curbs on immorality and personal selfishness, and without faith will soon fall, believes Billy Graham.

In 1 Corinthians 6:11 the apostle Paul—speaking about immoral relationships, sensuous living, and lack of control—reminds Christ's followers that "such were some of you," but now they had put away this kind of living. A faith in God and obedience to Him are needed by couples today.

Responsible marriage is still God's best plan for the highest human happiness and security for one man and one woman.

Mrs. Opal Lincoln Gee, a minister's wife of Springfield, Missouri, has had the courage to speak out about free love, and I share with you the entire article:

A Minister's Wife Speaks Out About Sex

I'm for marriage! I've read many prophecies that our social mores will change and have pondered the intensifying propaganda for so-called sexual freedom. Yet I'm still for marriage. I'm for the *freedom* of marriage. The prospect of having a dozen different love affairs during my life appalls me with its restrictions—and I say this after being married to the same man for nearly twenty-two years.

We may as well start with sex. Give me the liberty of the marriage bed. Give me the freedom of a sexual relationship with one lifetime partner. Give me the complete abandon of the physical and spiritual oneness found only in married love.

In marriage there is freedom from fear. How I'd hate to be hemmed in by the fears I know I'd feel in a transitory relationship. Improvements in birth-control methods have taken away much of the fear of conception. Still, thousands of illegitimate babies are born every year. Even in marriage the possible consequence of the mating act can at times inhibit a woman's response to it. Outside marriage, where

38

these fears are multiplied many times, what freedom could a woman enjoy?

There is also freedom from comparison. I am not troubled by a gnawing fear that I might not be living up to a former partner's performance. There is a satisfying security in the knowledge that I did not lure my husband from the embrace of another woman and because he, too, wholeheartedly believes in marriage, that no other woman can alienate him from me because her body is more seductive.

There is freedom to grow old within the comfort of my husband's love. I don't think I could bear the agony of being discarded when my physical capacities in this realm, as in others, lose the vigor of youth.

Marriage has made me a mother four times. I would hate to be an unmarried mother, and not only because it is still frowned upon by society. What glorious freedom there is in being able to share the joy of a baby's birth and growth with a husband, who usually feels the same pride and elation in this greatest of all joint enterprises. How fenced in I would have felt had I been required to act modestly with *everybody!*

There are countless memories of shared joys and sorrows in a good marriage. I'd hate being cheated of these. There have been hundreds of shared small triumphs and of private jokes that are funny only to us. It takes a while for a man and a woman to build up this kind of easy mental intimacy.

I am not bored but rather comforted by my knowledge of how my husband will react to almost any situation. I don't have to be tormented with self-doubts when he is quieter than usual; years of living with him have taught me that he is worried about something, not disenchanted with me. I wasn't always sure those first few years.

In marriage I find freedom to grow as a whole person. I don't think this would be possible for me with any relationship less intimate and binding. Be-

39

cause I don't have to be constantly concerned with my deduction rating, I have energies with which to pursue my interests and nurture whatever talents I have. No doubt this makes me more interesting to my husband. It certainly fulfills a deep need in me.

I think marriage also enriches my social life. I have more and better friends among both sexes than I could have as a single person. I consider many men my good friends. We have delightful conversations. I don't have to worry about impressing them, and they don't have to be wary of me!

I suppose monogamy is one kind of freedom and the "new morality" is another, and I grant that the price of marital freedom is high. One has to give up a great deal of selfishness in order to achieve peace and happiness with another person. I would not say that my husband and I were each the one perfect choice for the other. At times, we've felt madly incompatible! Yet the territorial rights and freedom of marriage have given us space to grow not only as separate beings but in an ever-deepening oneness that has brought us much happiness.

It has given life to four other happy human beings, too. I can't see how "free love" could ever produce this kind of happiness for people. No doubt, it satisfies physical passion. Yet I wonder how much tenderness you would find in a man unwilling to give his name to and sacrifice himself for his possible unborn child? How much real love is there in a woman concerned only with herself, her sex partner, and the thrill of the moment?

With America's emphasis on sex, it isn't any wonder that even very young people come to believe that sexual gratification is the "pearl of great price," worth the exchange of all other treasures. Unfortunately, by the time many of them find out that other treasures are highly valuable also, it is too late. They have thrown them away on somebody who doesn't know diamonds from rhinestones.

40

I believe that the God who made us gave us marriage because he knew it would bring us the highest happiness. Some call this naivete. Others consider it romanticism. To them I can only offer my own experience in reply: Marriage has brought great happiness to me.[1]

I for one sincerely respond, "Thank you, Mrs. Gee, for saying what so many of us have been wanting to say, but somehow couldn't find the right words to express ourselves as effectively as you have."

YOUTH DECEIVED

It is tragic to deceive young people today as some authorities are doing. Instead of giving proper guidelines and helps for unselfish and controlled living, they are rapidly pushing youth down the hill of moral decay.

Already we are aware of what is at the bottom of this hill. A recent report from New York states that sex is taking second place to drugs. Youth has explored and experimented in all there is to know about sex. It is old hat. They are tired of it, so now turn to drugs for kicks.

It seems to me that part of today's problem is that there is too much emphasis on the physical. It has become an end in itself, even in marriage.

Dr. Paul Popenoe, founder and president of American Institute of Family Relations in Los Angeles says, "Without fail—sex problems are solved when a couple does not focus on sex, but on other relationships: doing things together, respecting each other, consulting with each other, enjoying each other, working with personal faults, etc. As a result the couple's sexual partner becomes satisfactory to both."

We cannot deny it—marriage does bring with it

1. *Christianity Today*, Jan. 5, 1968, pp. 16-17. © 1968 by *Christianity Today;* reprinted by permission.

41

responsibility, limits, and discipline. But it brings many rewards—one of which is sexual freedom.

FREEDOM OF MARRIAGE

The freedom of marriage. That is it. Sex is free only in marriage. In marriage it becomes a symbol of unselfishness, concern, security, trust, and responsibility. These are characteristics of a happy, contented person.

God, the Producer, sent instructions along with His product, mankind. He limited the free expression of sex to the marriage relationship—not to deny us our rights, but that we might respect and enjoy its fruits *in the freedom of marriage*.

I join Mrs. Gee in speaking out for the freedom of marriage. How about you?

7

YOUR DAILY SCHEDULE

I HOPE you are enjoying your daily chores, because housework is here to stay!

Oh yes, it will be modified and made simpler in the future, just as it has in the past forty years, but it will never vanish.

And when a girl marries, she can expect two or three times more work taking care of husband, a home, and children!

Man sometimes gets out of work, and the family manages for a while, but let a woman get the idea of stopping her housework!

Well—I will skip the results.

LIKE IT

It is essential that you like to work—and you will, when you realize its supreme importance!

Many homemakers today admit they *hate* housework. But what surprises me is that they believe that the home and family do not suffer as long as they get the work done!

Dr. John Schindler, personal counselor and cofounder of the famous Monroe Clinic at Monroe, Wisconsin, says that it is bad enough to have to work, but it is ten times worse to work hard and long without liking it. That produces a trap. Having to work and not liking it "drieth up the bones," as the Bible puts it in Proverbs 17:22.

Dr. John Schindler adds, "It drieth up considerably more than the bones. It drieth up the humor, and the heart, one's mind, one's enthusiasm, pleasures, dreams; in short, one's living.

"Since you can't get out of housework, and since men have not yet gotten around to annihilating it, the trick, obviously, *is to learn to like work!*"[1]

IT IS IMPORTANT

Dr. Schindler then suggests that you learn to like it by finding an importance beyond yourself and the work. In other words, as you wash the dishes, dry the clothes, de-moth the closet, clean the baby, and wipe up messes, remember *why* these chores.[2]

You are making your husband happy and molding your children's characters—not only for time but for eternity!

That is why housekeeping is important! While your family lives, they need clothes, nourishing meals, a comfy home, your joy, and love!

The nationally-known marriage counselor, Paul Popenoe, says surveys conclude that housekeeping is a major factor in many marriage troubles. D. H. Lawrence said, "No woman does her housework with real joy unless she is in love."

Liking housework builds a happy home. That is your creation. You have made it such, of course, with the

1. *A Woman's Guide to Better Living* (New York: Prentice-Hall, 1957), p. 149.
2. Ibid.

cooperation of each family member. But you design, select the color, and fill in the stitches.

One homemaker decided that housekeeping chores would not trap her. She would use beautiful bowls, arrange flowers, and snatch a bit of beauty in each room. She thought, "Let your house, your work, your child be your satisfaction; they are already your choice."

After accepting this approach, she wrote, "Since that day my life has seemed invested with a tranquility I would scarcely have thought possible with four small children. Keeping house is not a trap. A woman who, by small but continuous effort, creates an atmosphere of contentment and order, where life may be simply enjoyed and lovely things are used for the pleasure they give in themselves, realizes her full potentiality. Her greatest possibilities for growth and contribution to society consist in transmitting learning, wisdom, order, and beauty, not to the world at large, but personally—by example mainly—to a few: her family."

MRS. FAIRFIELD

My good friend, Mrs. Norma Fairfield of Harrisonburg, Virginia, says she learned the hard way. But when once she became aware of the importance of housework, things happened in her home.

> I used to have hired help in our home three days a week. After I came to know the Lord, I realized this was not honest, since we didn't really need this much help . . . nor was it wholesome. There are few enough chores for children to do nowadays, and we were not learning how to live and work together as a family. So we made the change to no extra help at all.
>
> At first I tried to do all the work myself because I quickly found out that it took longer to show the

45

children how to do things than to do them myself. Soon I was exhausted and had no time for anything else but housework. So I asked the Lord to teach me.

He brought it to my mind to get a calendar with spaces for each day large enough to write in the daily chores and necessary activities . . . I still plan each week in this manner. As soon as I know about any meeting or similar activity any of us will be involved in, I mark it on the calendar. Then I mark down any special jobs for the week—like cookies for PTA, letter to Grandma, dental and doctor appointments, and so on.

I try to wash, iron, and bake on pretty much the same days each week, so no one runs out of clean socks or is left without a white shirt for a special occasion.

When the unexpected occurs or emergencies arise, and you have your week's duties laid before you like that, it's amazing how you can shuffle things around to accommodate all that really needs to get done. Much less frustrating and upsetting than trying to sort it out in your mind in the confusion of the emergency—much easier and less fraying to your nerves and those of your family!

The Lord has taught me the value of each child knowing what is expected of him. I assign certain chores to the children. The children have all made their own beds since kindergarten days. And they are responsible for keeping their bedrooms reasonably tidy. The boys help with the outdoor work—lawn, garden, carpentry. The girls with the inside work—ironing, cleaning, and baking—pretty generally. Although both will help outdoors and in, depending on the need.

They are expected to pick up after themselves. A houseful of people who never put anything back they've used or pick anything up they've dropped, can reduce a neat house to a shambles in a half hour or so. It takes cooperation to combat this kind of dis-

46

order and an earnest desire on the part of each one to do his or her part to have a neat home, and let's face it, a certain amount of "reminding."

The Lord says that our times are in His hand. I find that when I ask Him for wisdom in anything, including running a home and keeping it neat and clean, He is always true to His promise—He shows me how to do.

Your Schedule

In planning your daily schedule you will want to do like Norma: list all the chores—the daily, the weekly, the occasional ones, doctor and dental appointments, school and church activities. Then schedule them in your day's plans. And assign jobs to each child. After writing them down for some months, you may be able to plan much of the day's work in your mind. However, jot down on the calendar the special events and jobs.

Also allow time for your personal needs. Plan a rest period—to read, to meditate, to pray, and to relax. Plan special times with the family, and an occasional evening out with just hubby and you.

Let me emphasize this—your schedule must be only a guide. You dare not be married to it! It must be flexible, able to bend and stretch, to include the daily unexpected experiences—visitors, a fretful baby, sickness, husband's plan, or family picnic.

I think it is important that every homemaker plan a daily schedule, a guide, if you please, so that she can more efficiently do the necessary housekeeping chores. That way the "lesser" jobs, or what-I-want-to jobs, do not crowd out the "musts," and she gets done, not just stops late at night!

If housework is a drudge for you, ask God to remind you of its importance. Allow Him to help you plan your daily schedule.

After Breakfast Prayer

"Dear Father, now that my family
    has gone to work and to school,
    a sudden quiet falls on this disordered house.
Help me to face the work for this day
    with a singing heart—
    the dishes to wash, the beds to make,
    the clothes to launder, and the picking up
    which sometimes seems as futile as
    sweeping a forest floor in the time of falling leaves.
"I thank Thee: that I am needed,
    that my job in these busy years
    is to create a home that will be a
    place of warmth and comfort and love.
Help me to see each task, not as a dull chore,
    but as a strand woven into a pattern of living.
Grant I pray, that it may be a pattern to remember,
    a pattern of order, and beauty, and through
    it always may there gleam the golden thread
    of Christ's spirit.—Amen."

JOSEPHINE ROBERTSON

8

FIGHT FATIGUE

ARE YOU TIRED in the morning, before the day's work begins?

Fatigue may be caused by an organic ailment. But—you have checked with a competent physician and there is nothing wrong. And you are still always tired!

A BIG THREAT

According to industrial experts, chronic fatigue is one of the biggest threats to employee productivity—and advancement.

In the United States and Canada 40 percent of men in the 45-64 age group die of heart attacks. Only 7 percent in Japan and France. There the men know how to relax.

THE TIRED HOMEMAKER

Most of us mamas rush from the time we lift an eyelid in the morning until it stays put at night, rushing from serving breakfast, to washing, to tending the babes, to sweeping, to lunch, to fixing tricycles, to naps, and on until late at night. We find ourselves tired and weary, without taking one minute to relax!

No wonder the modern woman buys vibrating mattresses and chairs, and resorts to tranquilizers.

In the words of Samuel Butler, "Life is one long process of getting tired."

Too tired to care! If you are on your feet all day, tired feet wear you out, causing just plain fatigue and probably crankiness.

Or you may be tired from being at home all day doing nothing—nothing in your schedule to look forward to eagerly. A daily battle with fatigue and weariness, not from physical exercise, but from doing nothing!

In Shakespeare's play, *As You Like It,* Cymbeline says,

> Weariness can snore upon the flint,
> When resty sloth finds the down pillow hard.

Tiredness results from strenuous physical labor, from overwork. But normally a hard-working person will be refreshed after a night's rest. He or she will not wake tired.

Fatigue, then, seems to be more a state of mind, probably resulting from disgust for the job, or from criticism, or from rebellion, or lack of adjustment and contentment, or from pressures.

COMBAT FATIGUE BY DAYDREAMING

Now that we have thought about fatigue and its causes, let us think about some ways of fighting, or overcoming it—besides soaking in hot water.

Psychologist Jerome L. Singer, of Columbia University, suggests daydreaming. His study shows that frequent daydreamers are more resourceful, more creative. They have a greater capacity for original thinking.

But there is one thorn in this lovely rose! The daydreamer frequently lacks patience to plod along when the going gets tough. He usually looks for an easier way, for a shortcut, to making his dreams come true.

So, remember—you need to daydream a bit, but not too much.

BY WALKING

Walking helps you unwind. It is cheap, rewarding, and plentiful.

To be helpful, a walk should not have a destination or a set time for return. Walk for the sake of walking. Enjoy the surroundings. Give yourself the time to re-acquaint yourself with the earth, the sky, and the creatures at home there.

Walking is nearly magical medicine for a limp, weary, and bogged-down mind.

BY CHILDISHNESS

In Germany, psychologists have a different theory on how to relax and unbend—revert to childish play. That is, relive or reexperience one's childhood. As a result, a group of tense men and women in Munich have formed the Slapstick Club. Among other carefree, childish delights, they dress in old clothes and throw eggs, custard pies, and ripe tomatoes at each other!

Frankly, I am quite sure that if I reverted to such "unbending" tactics, I would develop new tensions and fatigue!

BY PHYSICAL TRAINING

Gosta Olander of Sweden has helped many people all over the world to relax and get fit. He believes that physical training is mental preparation as well as bodily exertion. "The ultimate springs of physical performance are not in the muscles, but in the mind. Exercise must be directed in helping nature." Olander's pupils include many world-famed athletes. But he also has a message for those confined to desks daily. Muscles stimulated by nervous tension bring on fatigue. So his solution is to reduce tension. He believes that man's nervous system is fighting a losing battle with the pressures of our advanced civilization.[1]

His prescription calls for long walks, preferably in the country. But I was happy to note that window-shopping will do! Coupled to this is close observing of one's surroundings, increasing awareness, and putting into perspective the complications of life.

BY RELAXING

Olander says animals are always fit because they stay relaxed, unless there is need for exertion in killing or escape. Their nerves do not continually battle with their muscles.

Yes, he also speaks to the housewife and office worker. A two-hour walk in the woods or along a lake shore relaxes nerves and muscles. If not two hours, then surely, not less than one hour. Anxiety is replaced by a feeling of calm as this refreshing daily habit takes hold.

Furthermore, Mr. Olander condemns a two-week vacation crammed into several days. Exercise that is valuable must be done in a relaxed state of mind. If not, the same condition producing fatigue in the factory, in the office, or at home, will produce it on vacations, on the golf course, or in the bowling alley.

Mothers used to push baby carriages and strollers in the park. I guess many still do today. Other mothers take almost daily unhurried walks with toddlers and older children. Although thinking only in terms of parental duty (the best for their children) they unconsciously have become better mothers because of this time for relaxation.

Seventy-six-year-old Emilio Jimenez, who, for fifty years has arranged healing vacations for fashionable

1. *Readers Digest,* August 1964, p. 76.

Europeans, reports that women no longer know how to go on healthy vacations.

He explained, "Men know enough to relax and do nothing, but women want to work hard, visiting museums, painting, dancing, shopping, and writing books. They must learn to relax."

We women must learn how to relax daily—not only on vacation. And every one of us *could* set aside ten or fifteen minutes (or longer) every morning and afternoon—a period in which to relax, to soak our feet, to meditate, or to walk unhurriedly out-of-doors.

JUST SIT

George Herbert, in the sixteenth century, said, "He that is weary let him sit."

So homemaker, pull out that easy chair and sit. Yes, just sit. And rock for at least five minutes. Name everything you are thankful for. Then pull out your mending and mend awhile, or pull that cranky toddler onto your lap and sing her a lullaby. Read, or play peek-a-boo, or pull out your Bible and read one or two verses. Meditate on them. What is hidden in them for you? For your family? For the community? For the church?

REST IN GOD

Jesus Christ invites you, "Come to me and I will give you rest—all of you who work so hard . . . let me teach you; for I am gentle and humble, and you shall find rest for your souls" (Matthew 11:28-30, *Living Bible*).

Yes, just stay sitting. Talk to Him; unload all your frustration, tension, weariness, concerns, sorrow, and disappointments—everything that is bogging you down. Tell God that restless living has caused you to lose your calmness. Tell Him about needless confusion, and an anxious heart. Ask Him to teach you His rewards of rest.

Wait before Him. Sit, and relax, and lose your fatigue.

Shall Not Faint

The woman who sits,
Whose spirit blends with Jesus,
Who waits on the Lord's message and guidance,
Shall soon get up and soar
Above her duties with wings of eagles.
She can run after the children
And not be weary;
She can keep up her daily homemaking tasks
And not faint;
For God gives courage
To the faint-hearted homemaker.
To the one who is a victim of chronic fatigue,
He gives *new* strength.

ELLA MAY MILLER

9

PLIGHT OR PRIVILEGE

A KANSAS HOUSEWIFE, Mrs. Mary Ann Noah, several years ago won the Powder Puff Derby. It was her second win in the annual women's transcontinental air race, because bad weather threw her competitor off course.

Frankly, I would rather weather the storms—with my two feet on the ground—while managing the daily family race to school, to work, and to where have you! But many housewives wish they did have wings and could soar above daily duties and tensions! They feel bound, discriminated against, or just plain frustrated with their career.

Here are several letters written to a newspaper editor, after he had published an article about the modern woman's search for meaning.

SELF-FULFILLMENT

A homemaker from Seattle, Washington, wrote:

> This selfish, grasping enthronement of "happiness" as the ultimate goal in life creates the "lives of quiet desperation" which it deplores. Happiness, by its nature, cannot be the goal; it is a by-product of a life which has escaped from the prison of self, a life in which responsibilities are accepted and duty is faced, not with inner reservations and resentments, but

55

gladly, in loving service. Love is the key—not love meaning sexual attraction, as it is too frequently misused today, but love meaning a deep and abiding concern for others with whom we share this crowded planet. This love is, of course, by the nature of man, deepened with proximity but can be extinguished by too much concern for self.

The life spent in pursuit of such an ideal is less likely to founder in the treacherous shoals of cynicism and despair than is the life spent in futile pursuit of the will-o-the wisps of "self-fulfillment" or "happiness."

I think this woman has dug down to grass roots. If the American woman is unfulfilled and frustrated when fulfilling her role as a woman, I think the trouble is somewhere else, not in the career God planned for her.

A clothes washer would do a poor job of washing dishes—even though you might want to use it for such! Similarly, God created us women for a unique role.

When we have *chosen* this role, and then run away from its responsibilities and privileges, we are about as efficient as a clothes washer washing dishes! We break lives, and soon need repairs ourselves.

GLAMOR

Not only has the word *fulfillment* made havoc of many lives, but a close runner-up is *glamor*.

An Illinois homemaker questions:

Why shouldn't women be dissatisfied? Just a look through the magazines or the stores will answer this.

Dresses, advertisements, displays, etc., are based on glamour. How does one scrub the floor in a beautiful, long, silvery house gown? Can we have the beautiful rugs and floors polished when the boys decide a baseball game be best played inside? Can't you just imagine a daintily coiffured lady, her long, polished nails, all her make-up denoting glamour, pointing the way out to some small, grubby boys as they point their ball to bring down the satin drapes?

But how does one get these gorgeous things the advertisements tell about, the leading magazines tell us every woman should have? Money for clothes, fancy furniture, home accessories, or jewelry must be earned. A second car, a color TV set can only be bought if both husband and wife work.

Industry can use a woman as well as a man. Not that she prefers to work—she has to work—she has to get what she wants.

No, woman's place has not changed. The economy has. The desires have.

I agree. Economy has changed. But, dare we women sacrifice our womanly desires of home, family, love, acceptance, and happiness for lesser things such as glamour, money, or possessions which are temporary and unfulfilling?

EMANCIPATION

Let us take up another word, *emancipation.*

Has emancipation brought happiness to the modern woman?

A Virginia woman wrote,

> Who's emancipated? The American woman is continually being less than a full-fledged citizen every day. For instance, let me point out that not until recently did anyone think to put the word *sex* in any wording of anything banning discrimination because of color, etc., and women have been bearing discrimination since mother Eve. Furthermore our present laws do not protect the women of this nation nor our homes.

She then cites a case where the law did not protect a divorcee who was not getting support from her husband.

Wrong Goals

At this point I ask, Aren't we focusing on wrong values—on purely selfish goals? Somehow we have failed to emphasize woman's role as helper to man (not his boss or competitor); woman's role as mother to mankind (not mother of gadgets, and of dogs).

It was refreshing to read about nineteen-year-old Jacquiline Gayraud, *Miss France* of 1964. She refused contracts as a model, starlet, or beauty queen for four years.

She explained that "A typical representative of French girlhood must obey her parents, and my parents want me to study domestic science for the next four years. They say that a woman cannot be attractive to a man for long if she does not know how to take care of him and his home."

I wish more American girls had this philosophy!

A Career

A Pennsylvania career woman, childless, and who as a nurse has counseled many young women, comments on the modern woman's search for meaning.

She has observed the young married woman—working until baby is born, then back on the job when the child is six weeks old. It is good for husband and wife to cooperate in buying house, car, groceries, and supplies, she writes,

> But when a baby comes I believe the mother should give up her work and be with that baby. Psychiatrists tell us there is no substitute for the tender, loving care of a mother and the security she brings in the formative years.
>
> In most, if not all, of the articles I have read, the emphasis has been placed on the woman and her marriage, with no mention of her responsibility as the very backbone of the family where the morals and the

58

stability of the child begin. Fortunately, I believe that the woman who does realize and assume this responsibility does not think of herself as a poor, frustrated homemaker but as fortunate in comparison to the career woman.

I will admit, when the dishes stack up, when the preschoolers all have measles, you tend to envy the women with jobs away from home.

But remember, all that glitters is not gold.

Religious Concept

A Utah housewife very nicely defines homemaking in her letter:

> I believe it to be an unfortunate situation when a woman finds herself frustrated and incomplete in her role as mother and wife. This feeling of monotony and despair need not exist in the mind of a woman if her thinking is beyond self. Self is crucified when people, male like female, have fellowship with Christ. When this religious concept is abandoned then there is an abundance of room within the individual for the growth of a number of maladies. Some of these take on the name of ingratitude, irresponsibility, neglect, unloving, temperamental, harshness, and selfishness.
>
> Instead of the woman placing on her life's menu what is best for her child or husband she fills it rather with a trite expression, "I'm bored."
>
> Woman will feel trapped and will be on the prowl as long as she is empty from within. A master's or doctor's degree cannot bring peace to the mind and soul. She can seek all means to escape her responsibilities as a mother and wife only to discover in later years that she forsook the blessings of womanhood for extra income or prestige.
>
> Paul Foley wrote of the successful professional women in the USSR. Success in a profession isn't

59

nearly as outstanding as is success in meeting the high standards of motherhood. Is Mr. Foley advocating that all you working mothers unite, for you have nothing to lose but your children?

Would I want my child to be subjected to another's teaching and guidance daily when I knew that the keeper of my child has misplaced values? I would not. I believe that I am best qualified to tend to my child's needs of love, understanding, and companionship. And as long as I am able to do so, I will do so, and I will consider it a vast privilege heaped on so much pleasure. I have been charged by God to meet my responsibilities as a mother and wife, and there are still many hours left in the day for self-improvement and mental advancement—only the desire is needed.

THE SECRET

This homemaker has touched the core of modern woman's dilemma.

Joy and fulfillment in homemaking depend on you, not on the job.

God created woman for a unique role: to bring comfort, courage, concern, and love to man, to children, and to society as a whole. This should be her palace—not her prison.

I ask, "Has modern woman's dream of *privilege* and of *rights* boomeranged into her *plight*?"

10

CONTENTMENT IS GREAT GAIN

ONE NATIONAL HOLIDAY I especially enjoy is Thanksgiving Day. I am thankful that our government recognizes the importance of gratitude and endorses this day.

Perhaps my appreciation of the day goes back to memories of Thanksgiving Day celebrations during my childhood and youth.

THANKSGIVING DAY

The day before Thanksgiving, we celebrated at school with a special program. Thursday and Friday were vacation days, when we children enjoyed many fun things.

Thanksgiving morning we attended a church service, an informal type of singing and saying thanks to God for all His blessings. Some of those days were during the dust bowl years. But somehow the feeling got through to me that the people were grateful. Then we returned home to a special dinner.

In the afternoon some of the men and boys went hunting. We children played leisurely.

NEED REMINDER

I am aware that this day is not magic. It will not make me a thankful person, if during the remaining 364 days of the year I am a chronic complainer.

But, I need the reminder to count my blessings, to be grateful and thankful in the midst of abundance.

It is good to remember that years ago our forefathers were grateful for a crop of corn, and for wild turkeys, grateful enough to leave their work for one day and gather together to worship and thank God.

Gratitude is the foundation upon which contentment is built.

"NOBLE DISCONTENT"

When I mention contentment, I also need to mention false contentment.

You should not be satisfied or content with the status quo, with social conditions such as poverty, war, discrimination, ill will, greed, graft, hate, vice. You should not be content with your own failures, weaknesses and sins, or your child's illness. In these experiences you need a noble discontent.

An undercurrent of noble discontent should drive you to help relieve needy persons, and to search for a new life of joy, love, and peace in Jesus Christ, to be a kinder, more understanding wife, a happier mother, more loving, more patient, more forgiving.

Nor should you ever be content with your accomplishments. But be content with what you have now, content with your situation today, which you cannot control.

CONTENT DEFINED

The word *content* is derived from a Latin word meaning "to hold together." So basically *contentment* does not mean to be resigned. Neither does it mean complacency. It is being held together. This, of course produces satisfaction.

Now let us think of the negative, to clarify the word a bit more. Discontent is without content. You are no holding together. You are disorganized, and therefore, unsatisfied.

When you are content your thoughts are holding together in the situation where you find yourself. You think clearly. You keep in focus true values of life. As a natural result, you think, talk, and act in an organized manner.

CONTENT WITH SELF

Self-contentment is very important! In a disorganized, upset world, you need to hold together. You begin with yourself. You exist as you are, so accept yourself. Hold together with who you are—with your unique personality, with the talents and qualities God gave you or did not give you.

You are *you*—not Susy or Mary—nobody else, just you.

If you chose marriage, you are a wife—not a single girl.

If you have a child, you are a mother—not childless.

Or you may be a pianist—not an artist.

Possibly you are an interior decorator—not a cosmetic saleslady.

You are organized, holding together, content to the degree you accept your unique self, your personhood.

CONTENT WITH CIRCUMSTANCES

You also need an attitude of contentment with those circumstances you cannot change. Some women have told me how they achieved this attitude.

Lois says she is often tempted to feel sorry for herself. They moved on an average of every three years, for nineteen years, because of her husband's work.

"We know what it is to be with different types of people in various communities and churches. . . . We have never regretted our moves because they are always promotions. I'm sure our girls can adjust to situations that maybe some couldn't because of our many experiences in moving."

Lois is content—not because everything is rosy, but because she has accepted herself as an individual person, as the wife of a man who occasionally moves, and as a mother of teenagers.

No Complaint

Mrs. B. believes that contentment with what she has is the greatest of all riches! She wrote:

"God has helped me every day. I was left a widow five years ago, with seven children. . . . I was in debt ten thousand dollars. So I decided to find work. I have been doing housework ever since. I drive forty-two miles a day to and from work. I am fifty-seven years old. I believe in prayer. I don't receive any help at all except my Social Security check. I have prayed that I would be able to take over the burdens alone. So far I have. I am almost out of debt."

Imagine—not a word of complaint!

I am reminded of Benjamin Franklin's proverb: "Content makes poor men rich; discontent makes rich men poor."

Count Blessings

Sandra tells how she got herself together.

One evening she had had it. She was very depressed and dissatisfied and wanted to escape from taking care of the preschool girls. She again envisioned using her English major in some other way than by reading "The Three Bears."

So after the girls were asleep, she decided to sort their baby clothes.

As she handled each dress, her mind went back to interesting happenings when the girl wore it.

Of course, you can guess what happened. By the time she was through, she was thanking the Lord for the girls. Not only was she rejoicing, but she went back to the pile of outgrown clothes she was giving away, and included some new dresses for the destitute girls whose eyes haunted her from a magazine.

Counting your blessings helps get rid of discontent.

Count your blessings, name them one by one,
And it will surprise you what the Lord hath done
JOHNSON OATMAN, JR.

DISCONTENT IS TRAGIC

If a woman does not count her blessings she becomes dissatisfied, and discontent often drives a woman to unnecessary demands and to excessive installment buying. This in turn may lead a husband to moonlighting, and then result in family troubles.

Kate complained about her house until Tom bought a new one. Then he took on two jobs to meet the payments. He was never home, it seemed. Soon she began accusing him of not caring for her. She made the few minutes he was at home so miserable for him, that he was glad to leave again. Instead of changing her attitude, she blamed him for her unhappiness. Within two years she married the fellow next door.

Gail's discontent took her out of the home to earn money for things she wanted but did not really need. Her children, six and ten, were neglected. She left them to shift for themselves. Today, they are juvenile delinquents. The parents are heartbroken.

Many times the result is the same—a broken home and ruined lives—because of discontent.

LEARN CONTENTMENT

You can learn to be content. This is the way it works.

Instead of griping because you do not have this or that, or you cannot do something, bring to mind something you have, something you can do, something you do enjoy. It boils down to changing your thoughts.

Instead of thinking about all the things you do not like, think on what you do appreciate. Focus on these. In every area of your life you need to focus on your blessings.

Mary says when she is tempted to compare her husband with another, she starts thinking about his kindness, his love, and his faithfulness to her. Perhaps he is not as good looking as some—so what?

A grateful person is a contented person. Gratitude is the foundation upon which contentment is built.

CONTENTED PARENT

We parents need to be examples of contentment for our children. This is especially true for us mothers, because we set the tone, the atmosphere, in the home.

Contentment brings happiness, an inner joy, and peace of mind. It frees your mind for positive, worthwhile thoughts and actions.

Homemaker, are you content?

Take a good look at your gripes. Analyze them. Face reality. Focus on true values of life. Accept God's love—His concern, love, and interest in you, through Jesus Christ.

Just turn your life over to Him, and let Him fill you with His joy and peace and love. Let Him help you organize your thoughts, help you think about the good, the true and worthwhile. And be thankful. God wants to show you how to fit yourself into every situation. If there is no need to change, just accept it. Hold yourself together.

Be content!

11

ACCEPTING DIFFICULTIES

How is your control?

How do you react to that impossible situation? Possibly you are facing one right now.

I am told that the dinosaurs became extinct because they could not adjust to the changing climate.

A world of fast-changing tempo forces new and difficult situations upon us. They frustrate many of us today.

Difficulty and trouble become intolerable, like a screw being steadily and remorselessly turned tighter. Men and women feel that everyone and everything is against them. They are ready to quit.

Is there a successful treatment for embitterment, a remedy for fear and lack of courage?

I would like to share with you ways of being able to accept difficulties and to meet them positively.

FAITH MUST BE PRACTICAL

I have a simple answer. Trust in God. Indeed, faith and confidence in a loving heavenly Father are most necessary. However, I will quickly add that faith must be lived out in daily life—must become practical.

One frustrated, unhappy mother believes in God, yet, she is on the verge of a nervous breakdown, simply because she cannot harmonize her acts with her belief. Her only daughter had to marry the young man she had been dating. At seventeen years of age, when other girls are in high school enjoying life, this girl is far away from loving parents and friends. She is cramped in a small apartment caring for a husband and a baby.

The mother is heartbroken. She spends most of the day in bed, weeping and blaming herself.

GERALDINE AND JOE

Geraldine was lost in the cloud of despair and self-pity because of a drunkard husband, Joe.

One day she realized that Joe was hopeless. She would have to stop pitying herself. So she decided to continue making a home for Joe, but let the police look after him. She would make her children's lives and her own as cheerful and happy as possible.

She became cheerful, planning projects for the children. She found work to do at home with the children helping. Because of limited finances, their enjoyment was inexpensive. They became able to enjoy little things. Geraldine redecorated her half-wrecked furniture. All of them became active in Sunday school and other activities.

All this was not easy. But when Geraldine changed her attitude from self-pity to one of courage, she changed.

Formerly a melancholic complainer and careless about her appearance, she is now an attractive and very enjoyable person.

Geraldine first accepted that which she was powerless to change—she was married to a drunkard. At the same time, she took herself in hand and with courage, faith, and optimism she changed those conditions she could change.

Courage is not the absence of fear but the mastery of it.

I am also reminded of Helen, a missionary friend of mine. After three years in India, she contracted polio. Her baby was only eight months old. She was flown home in an iron lung. Progress has been slow and difficult. Although unable to run her wheelchair, she reviews books, does art work, and types on an electric typewriter. Her triumphant story has appeared in her autobiography, *Through Sunlight and Shadow*. She continues to write and has authored several books.

My niece is a polio victim of fifteen years. She is scarcely able to turn over in bed without help. Yet she graduated with honors from high school, won a scholarship to college, and is employed locally. I was privileged to spend most of a day with her, and not once did she complain about anything. Not once! Her eyes glowed with contentment and joy as she told me of her happy school year, discussed her paintings and awards, and demonstrated her new, lovely stereo set.

I am sure you know of those around you who have faced a difficult situation and have happily risen above it. It is all in their attitude, the way they take it. True courage is like a kite—a contrary wind raises it higher.

THOSE WHO FAILED

You can probably think of someone who couldn't take it. My mind carries me to the home where the mother is bedfast, simply because she would not accept the fact of a handicapped child. Another mother once was lovely and well-liked, but today she pays no attention to her personal appearance. She refuses to leave her home because her child is disfigured.

I am thinking also of the wife who has literally hounded her husband to death because of financial reverses. She can talk only of the days when money was abundant. Again, it is all in the attitude of these people. No doubt they know what should be done but do not know how.

ACCEPT THE FACT

Dr. John Schindler suggests that in learning to accept adversity, you should sometime plan how you would act if a great calamity should come upon you.[1] In just thinking, you will create a great emotional response. Your breath will come hard. Your heart will beat faster, and your head will feel woozy.

You cannot avoid such feelings. They will come, and to a much greater degree should something like death to your husband or child, or financial loss actually come to you.

Now starting at this point, you can work out your own approach to such a situation. But first, you must accept the fact. Instead of becoming hysterical or screaming, "It can't be! I won't believe it!" you will have to admit it is true. Then you must say, "I can meet this situation with God's help."

DECIDE ON SOMETHING GOOD

Now you will need to use the attitude that will let you rise above the terrible reality. You must decide on something good that can carry you to victory.

After one young mother faced her husband's sudden death, she said, "Paul was a wonderful man. It was a great privilege to have been able to live with such a person. I guess it's up to me now to give these children the same wonderful spirit he always would have given them . . . and I'm going to keep him and his influence here by trying to be as he would have been." And that is exactly what she did.

1. *A Woman's Guide to Better Living,* p. 71.

I have intimated that your attitudes, your thoughts about difficulties make the difference. This is true as you accept the facts. Furthermore, you must expect sudden and serious changes as normal.

A hymn writer says, "Chance and change are busy ever, worlds decay and ages move." But he adds that God never changes. God is our refuge, our shelter. In His arms we find protection and help.

You can also condition yourself for change and difficulty by not being one who always has done it this way and always will. Turn the hopeless, aggravating situation into a joke as you roll out your sense of humor.

Always find and play up the compensations. When the unchangeable happens, jot down all the possible benefits from such a situation. Meditate on these. Use your disappointments as opportunities for happiness and success. Remember to change the *d* to *h*, which reads, "His appointments." Be thankful that it was not any worse.

Even death can cause thanksgiving if the individual was prepared to meet God. Yes, thanksgiving! Because pain and suffering are ended.

Daily Difficulties

For most of us, there come the unchangeable daily situations which we must face. They are quite trivial in comparison to those I have mentioned. Oh, it might be sickness. It might be Saturday, and you are up to your neck in catching up with odds and ends of the week. Suddenly the electricity goes off for several hours. Can you still retain a calm and cheerful disposition?

"God grant to me the serenity to accept the things I cannot change, the courage to change the things I can, and the wisdom to know the difference," is a prayer taken from the writings of St. Francis of Assisi.

71

I think this little prayer, breathed many times daily, will help us homemakers to rise above our immediate difficulties. In doing so, we unconsciously give strength and courage to our husbands and children.

COURAGE FOR THE FUTURE

I am thinking just now of our nation's future. Can the United Nations guarantee peace? Will our nation continue to advance under its new leadership? These may be mountain-high difficulties that you see.

But remember, God is still at the controls. The Bible says that He places in authority those whom He will. He knows the end from the beginning. His supernatural strategy is faultless. Just leave it all to His good judgment. Yes, indeed, with Him you *can* face the future with courage.

Take courage. You do not need to stumble, although your path is dark as night. Just trust God. He will lead you right.

IT WORKS

In my short life, God has designed many changes— many insurmountable difficulties. Had I been given advance notice of them, I would have cried, "Impossible!" Yet through each situation, God has given me thoughts and attitudes of encouragement and happiness. I had to *learn to be* content and accept the situation just as I found it. I repeat, I had to learn. Sometimes the learning process was slow and painful. I could see only the wrongs, the hurts. But I eventually remembered that with God things do not just happen. He overrules every detail in the life of the one who loves Him. I also found that His grace, His loving concern, was sufficient to enable me to rise above the difficulty.

It is possible to know what you should do, and yet not do it. Here is where we need God. He helps us to do what we know we should. He gives us the power, the *will* to think rightly, to form right attitudes.

The Bible says that no matter what happens in any situation, be joyful in the Lord. Discuss with God each detail of the difficulty, how it affects you and your family. Tell Him how you had hoped conditions would be. Consult Him on all details. Tell Him that you are thankful it is not worse. Then ask Him to show you your next step. Draw from Him courage and power to do that which He suggests.

Mother, "Be strong! Be courageous! Do not be afraid of your difficulties! For the Lord your God will be with you. He will neither fail you nor forsake you." (Deuteronomy 31:6, paraphrased).

12

FUN TO LIVE WITH

"MY WIFE'S FUN to live with," says Roger, "because she's enthusiastic about life. I like it. She's excited and eager to have me home at five o'clock, and she shows it."

A woman can enjoy life.

Dr. John A. Schindler says, "Your disposition is the most important single factor for living enjoyably, regardless of whether you are rich or poor, smiled or frowned upon by fortune."[1]

A sure way to make yourself and everyone you live with miserable is to have a lousy disposition. A pleasant disposition helps make disagreeable situations bearable. It attracts your friends and family to you.

DISPOSITION IS ACQUIRED

Basically, in childhood you acquired the disposition of your family. Dispositions are handed down from generation to generation.

Some unpleasant dispositions are learned from the philosophy that we should never inhibit our impulses. You feel nasty when you get up, so you have to be honest and snap at everybody. You feel sarcastic, so you are sarcastic.

1. *A Woman's Guide to Better Living,* p. 25.

I believe I should express how I feel. If not, I develop hostility and build up resentments. However, expressing my feelings is simply stating, "I feel lousy—irritable, angry at the world. You'd better get out of my way." It is *not* making nasty, unkind statements to my family, breaking bottles, or slapping hands and heads.

You cannot be an uninhibited parent, nor allow your children to be uninhibited. Such a person develops many more conflicts with those to whom he relates. At the same time, you cannot just do or say anything you feel like. You need to express feeling rightly.

As an adult you can no longer blame your sour disposition on your parents and your childhood. Each woman lives in a world of her own. You have the power to make it a good one for your family, or a bad one. You can be happy in it, if you want to be happy, and know how to develop joy, peace, and happiness.

A PHILOSOPHY OF LIFE

Again quoting Dr. Schindler: "A good disposition is based on a certain philosophy of life. . . . [It] runs something like this. It is a good feeling just to be alive."[2]

Learn to love life. That means for you a woman's life. Accept yourself as a woman—in the life you have chosen. If you are a homemaker, say to yourself—many times today—"I'm important. I have a special place to fill by just being a woman."

Daily you can find delight and amazement in the success and accomplishments of your husband, of each child, of other people, of your own.

You can enjoy life when you remember that there is no perfect person, perfect house, or perfect day. You have to accept some bad with the good. Which you decide to concentrate on determines whether or not you enjoy life.

2. Ibid., p. 35

The small trifles are not worth getting upset about. The bigger difficulties can be met with courage, with a calm faith in God's plan and purpose for you. You will need enthusiasm about your daily tasks and privileges.

A kind sense of humor helps. Laugh at yourself. See the funny side of the children's spills and messes. Enjoy their interruptions, their clever remarks, their profound insight.

Learn to laugh when your husband locks the keys inside the car, when he calls home for the forgoten wallet or grocery list. Agree with him when he gives helpful criticism or observations.

You can find joy in the little things that belong to a homemaker's life.

You can find joy in helping someone else have a better day. This begins in the family circle.

GROWTH

You become an interesting person and fun to live with as you continue your growth intellectually—by reading, by learning a hobby, by entering into your husband's life and work, into your children's activities and interests. Also grow in your aesthetic appreciation—observe the color in the sunrise, sunset, clouds, flowers. Observe your child's glowing face as he brings you the dandelion flower, or later, as he introduces the new girl friend.

Grow in cultural interests. Be informed of what's available in your neighborhood. Grow by becoming interested in others.

I questioned Wayne about what makes his wife fun to live with. His face beamed, "Oh, she always has surprises and suggestions for the weekend to keep it from becoming drab—like driving across the mountains or visiting some historical spot. Or like this week, we're taking one of her pupils along to see the countryside."

Bring Happiness into Your Home

Mirth is not silliness or laughter due to dirty jokes, sarcasm, ridicule of a person, or laughing at mistakes. Not that! It is exuberance. It is a joy springing from within that expresses itself in fun, optimism, and laughter. It is laughing with people, not at people.

Help your child to be happy.

Marilyn is a polio victim, helpless from her shoulders down, but I have always been amazed at her cheerful disposition. She has a smile for everyone.

Recently I learned Marilyn's secret. Her mother related how when her girls were babies she would capture a smile, a happy moment, and remark, "You're happy, honey."

When they awoke from their naps she'd question, "Are you happy?" "As soon as they could talk," the mother remarked, "the girls would awaken and call from their cribs, 'I'm happy, Mama!' "

The Gift of Laughter

Sam Levenson, the TV humorist, believes the gift of laughter should be given to every child. He says that fun should be a part of the family diet.

His mother taught him his jovial manner. When he was nine years old, one day he received two whippings—one from the candy store man whose window his ball broke, and the other from his father. So Sam decided to revolt. Determined, he grabbed a can of sardines, wrapped a jersey top and pajama bottoms in a towel, picked up a road map of the US and Canada, and rushed to the front door.

His mother asked where he was going. He shouted, "Running away from home!"

She answered, "Wait, I'll call a taxi." Then he started to laugh. His brothers laughed. The neighbors began laughing. His plans changed. His mother's sense of humor had shown him how ridiculous his idea was.[3]

GOOD MEDICINE

Laughing is good medicine. That is what the Good Book says. Medical science proves this. Tests reveal that laughter has a tonic effect on 95 percent of all people. When you laugh your diaphragm goes up and down. This movement massages the right side of the heart, which increases the rate of your heartbeat, providing your body with a stimulating lift.

Mr. Levenson says his mother put humor into their hurts. When he cut himself accidentally, she would reply, "The best treatment for that is a chocolate cookie, but a Band-Aid will help."

She added fun to their work by placing a penny in the room he was to dust and then saying, "Find all the pennies in the dusty places, Sam."

Sam and his wife have taught their children responsibility and obligation. They have also brought in humor and laughter so the youngsters "see and feel that life has more sunny spots than clouds."

He jokes and plays funny games with his children before bedtime, and they sleep soundly. He suggests the following.

FUN-TIME RULES

1. Don't feel that you must do an act or a show every time you want your children to follow a simple direction. Humorous approaches invariably pay off when you teach youngsters something in a good-natured way—in a way that will stick to their memory and consciousness.
2. To develop a child's sense of humor, you must stimulate, and then join the fun at *his* level. It's out of place to hand adult humor to a six-year-old.

3. *Everyman's Family Circle,* February 1960.

3. Common sense is as important as humor in dealing with children. A novel way of handling some basic childhood problem may be most effective in your family. Don't be afraid to be original.

4. Remember that insult humor is not real humor. It's easy to stimulate a child's laughter by encouraging him or allowing him to tease other children. Or to make fun of their shortcomings and physical defects. But that is a harmful sort of laughter. When he laughs at another child with big ears, say this: "When you make fun of that child, you are making fun of God."

5. Apply a sense of humor in your attitude to your own life, and to your relations with your marriage partner. When facing problems, remember that humor is an important balance wheel.[4]

From Within

Laughter belongs to a pleasant disposition. Your disposition comes from within.

Eugenia Price says, "A woman's disposition is merely an outward sign of what she really is within. . . . If she is predominate there, her disposition shows it. If Christ is predominate there, her disposition shows that too."[5]

The joy and delight that lasts, no matter what, is found in being in tune with your maker, God. With Him, despair, depression, and despondency give way to optimism, joy, fun, laughter, and goodwill.

A happy, laughing family attracts others to their faith, to Jesus Christ. After all, joy is a fruit of the Holy Spirit.

Are you fun to live with?

4. Ibid., p. 60.
5. *Woman to Woman* (Grand Rapids: Zondervan, 1960), p. 21.

13

FAITHFUL IN LITTLE

In 1960, Eileen Farrell made her long-awaited debut at the Metropolitan Opera when she was already forty years of age. The only reason she had arrived at this late age was because her career was secondary to her interest in her children and husband.

Five years previously, Eileen had been asked to perform in France. She refused because it meant being away from home a month. "I can't leave my kids that long. Besides, who will iron Bob's shirts?"

It was encouraging to read about her dedication to her career as homemaker. What would happen in your community and mine if every wife and mother give homemaking top priority?

HOMEMAKING IS DIFFICULT

Sometimes we homemakers get bogged down with difficult situations. We begin to feel that they are ours alone. There is the temptation to feel that our responsibilities are too difficult. Green-eyed we watch the stenographer, the factory worker, the teacher. We make ourselves believe that their tasks are easier and more attractive.

In a sense there is something to this. There are occasions when we are at a loss to know how to handle the children's troubles and quarreling, even their teasing.

Just to illustrate: on a trip, we as a family were playing the alphabet game, that is, trying to find all the letters in proper order from the billboards. During an interval between games the nine-year-old asked her brother, "Why, didn't you see that X back there in Zoorama?" It was only a slip of the tongue, but you can just imagine that three brothers did not let her forget it during the remainder of the trip!

It is much easier and simpler to make an erasure in a typing error, or to correct errors in other jobs than to properly handle such errors in children's talk and play, creating a harmonious atmosphere.

It is a real temptation to make ourselves actually believe that a mother's job is more than we are capable of. Many such mothers then evade their duties. They do not consciously learn how to meet them successfully.

This mothering business does not come naturally. It requires dedication to the task. It requires knowledge, too, of what is necessary for happy, successful mothering. It takes courage and strength which only God can give so that we do what we know we should do.

HOMEMAKING INSIGNIFICANT?

There is also another temptation which faces every homemaker—that is to feel that her job is insignificant and mediocre. This, I believe, comes from considering only housework, the physical part of homemaking. To erase such attitudes, we need to emphasize the greatness of the task of a wife and mother, to stress those eternal rewards and intangible values.

If we do not ponder on these, we get all wrapped up in self-pity and resentment. All we are able to see is the daily routine—cooking and washing dishes three times a day, cleaning floors, doing laundry, dusting, making beds. I repeat, we are apt to focus our thoughts on these chores that are daily routine. It is a dangerous level on which to live!

But I would like to think with you how even *this* level of homemaking can be enjoyable. The modern split-level homes are beautiful. Each level contains a different group of rooms serving different family needs. Yet each floor is attractive and enjoyed by the homemaker. Well, just so in homemaking; there are different levels, yet each one can be beautiful.

KAREN'S MENDING

Karen pulled her chair up to the sewing machine, lifted the shirt from the top of the mending pile, and spread it out in front of her. She laughed, "Well, I guess one more patch and this will go to the rag pile." She found matching material and cut the exact size for a patch. For a few short minutes her needle swiftly flew in and out of the material, leaving small, neat stitches. Soon Karen folded the mended garment and placed it on the table beside her.

She next picked up a sock. Placing her hand inside it she found the small hole in the toe. "Hmmm, not very big, but 'a stitch in time saves nine.' " She darned the sock. And the next one. She sewed on buttons, mended tears in little dresses, and patched knees on boys' jeans. As she worked, Karen sang softly. Occasionally she would glance out of the window and feast her eyes on God's great out-of-doors. She let her mind wander to her husband's kindness and his love for her. She thought about the latest accomplishments of her four young children.

As she finished the last piece, the doorbell rang and in walked her next-door neighbor, Ann.

And she flopped herself on a chair, "Oh, this morning's been one grand mess! I thought the children would never get to school! They couldn't find their coats and scarfs. And then when they were gone, I had all the dirty dishes to do. I didn't even make the beds. There's the huge pile of ironing that's been stacking up these weeks."

Ann stopped to catch her breath. She ran her hand over the pile of mended clothes. "How in the world do you do it?"

Karen looked up at her, "You know, I used to try to squirm out of mending. Or leave it until Jake and the children didn't have any more socks to wear. But now I schedule this for Wednesday morning. It's fun to put the clothes back into the drawers before the family demands them."

Ann sighed, then asked, "But aren't you bored? And don't you think it's a waste of time to be darning socks? I just throw the kids' away when the holes get too big. I can pick up new ones at the dime store."

Karen smiled, "I try to think how pleased the youngsters will be to see the holes darned. Children enjoy the familiar and like to wear their old socks. I also keep reminding myself that 'a penny saved is a penny earned.' And besides, this gives me a bit of relaxation from the heavier tasks."

Ann ran her finger through her hair, "All right, that's mending. How about cleaning floors, and washing dishes, and repeating them daily, don't these get you down?"

Karen gave her sweetest laugh, "They used to. One day I discovered that these little things were big and important. Now I tackle these jobs and get them done instead of daydreaming about the glamorous and the unreal. I also learned, Ann, that I could be faithful in these little tasks and do them for the Lord. It's strange but true, since I enjoy the little things, I've been able to do bigger things for my family and for the community.

I guess God couldn't trust me with the bigger things before."

THE LITTLE THINGS ARE IMPORTANT

Karen learned an important truth, one that carries over not only into mending and routine housework, but into every area. Our lives, and our children's lives, are composed of lots of little things piled on to each other which result in big things.

Karen knew that mending a little hole meant longer service from the article of clothing. She knew that saving a little on many items would result in a big saving. Many single stitches make a new dress. Many single pennies make dollars.

Karen learned the principle that Jesus taught His followers—unless we are faithful in the little things, we cannot be entrusted with greater responsibilities.

CHILDREN NEED TO LEARN

How our children need to learn this! Too many youngsters want to be the leaders of their classes and school organizations. They want to be in the limelight, but they fail to do well the everyday little jobs. It is up to us to teach them the value of those smaller, unnoticed things—mending the snag, watching the pennies, cleaning up their plates, utilizing clothing and equipment until worn out. We need to teach them to work. To study, not "with eye service, as menpleasers," but with one purpose, that of pleasing the Lord.

LITTLE BY LITTLE

It is the little things, too, that form your child's character. Honesty is a result of many little things in the child's daily life.

In the book entitled, *A Penny's Worth of Character*,

little Shan's mother asks him to take empty sacks to the store and buy the groceries. Shan is happy, because he may keep the penny the grocer gives for each perfect sack. He counts them. There are only nine. He needs ten in order to buy a lemon soda and a candy bar. So he cheats and sticks in one with a tiny hole.

The grocer does not find the faulty one. Shan gets his soda and candy. When he arrives home his mother discovers his act. She sends him back to the store with a penny to pay the grocer. It was a bitter pill. Shan did not want to face the man. He did not want to walk those miles in the hot sun. But his mother insisted.[1]

Obedience is taught through a series of little things.

Two-year-old Susy runs away from the table. Mother says, "Susy, come back here. You don't leave the table until you finish eating." She may come at the first call, or she may not. But unless Susy's parents kindly but firmly see that she does come back, she will not learn obedience. And another thing, they must be consistent at every meal.

FAITHFUL WITH WHAT WE HAVE

I have heard mothers, and I suppose you have too, who constantly lament, "Oh, if I only had another house! Oh, if I only had nicer furniture, I could keep my home neater! Oh, if we only had more money, I could dress the children nicer! If we lived in another community, I could do something big." But, these same mothers are negligent and careless with what they do have.

GOD'S REQUIREMENT

The Bible says that God holds each one of us responsible for what we do have. This includes time, money, possessions, our children, our homes. He has loaned

1. Jesse Stuart (New York: McGraw, 1961).

them all to us for our brief journey here on earth. We are stewards of them.

Eventually we will give account to Him of how well we used our possessions. We will also give account of how well we trained our children. We will give an account to Him how well we fulfilled each joy He has assigned us.

God is considerate and fair. He does not demand of you what you do not have, or cannot do. All He asks is that you are faithful in what you do have. As we prove trustworthy in little things, He can then entrust us with bigger and greater things.

"He who is faithful in a very little thing is faithful also in much" (Luke 16:10, NASB).

Remember, mother, it is the little things in life that count. God expects you to be faithful.

14

OVERCOME HOUSEWIFE RESENTMENT

A HOMEMAKER shares her experience:

I was fed up, three children in twenty-two months and another on the way! Diapers, bottles, baby food, and screaming babies! Life consisted of one round after another of washing, ironing, and cleaning.

I had worked as a nurse before our marriage and had led a gay, carefree life. Now this. Not that I wanted to go back to nursing, but how could I stand this drudgery?

I longed to go places and do things—anything, anywhere—just to get away from the confining walls of my home. I was developing a good case of what mothers call "going house crazy."

"Take me out to dinner tonight," I begged my husband when he came home from work, even though I knew we couldn't afford it.

My husband, relaxing in an easy chair, answered, "I've been out all day. What's wrong with home?"

My mother had taught me never to let anything get me down, to always stay on top of circumstances, but now I found myself in a situation with which I was unable to cope. I couldn't take it—much less stay on top!

Twice I walked out on my family. I'd had it! I

couldn't stand another minute! But I didn't stay away more than a few hours.

My husband sympathized with me up to a point, but what was so bad about being a housewife? He told me I had a persecution complex. I had to admit to myself that he was right.

Sunday nights my husband agreed to babysit while I went to church. Maybe that would do some good.

Our own church didn't have Sunday evening services, so I chose a little church across town. Just getting away from the babies for an evening seemed glorious even if going to church didn't particularly excite me.

During these difficult days God was speaking to me. All my life I had regarded Him as a kind Father way off somewhere who was more or less looking after me. But I hadn't needed Him very often. I felt I was able to take care of myself, though I knew I was going to snap if I didn't get rid of my resentments. Gradually I came to realize that I was fighting God's plan for my life. Something kept drawing me back to the little church. Now I know it was *Someone*.

Baby number four had made his appearance in our home just before tragedy struck.

Our two-year old boy wandered off one day while I was busy washing clothes and caring for the new baby. I looked for my toddler in the wrong direction. By the time I had retraced my steps and started out the other way, my little son was already floating face down in the lake.

Only a mother can realize the feelings of loss, guilt, and heartache I experienced when my baby died. But at last I began to seek for the true values of life— began to think of the hereafter, of God. The Bible says, "A little child shall lead them." My little son led me, by his death, to God.

One day I dropped to my knees and committed myself and my family to the Lord. Jesus met me that day. He seemed so near, I felt I could touch the hem of His garment. I sincerely committed my problems to Him and attempted to accept the role He had given me as a mother.

My problems remained basically the same—diapers, bottles, messes to clean up, noise, work from dawn until I fell into bed at night. But now I had Someone to whom I could go for strength. I could talk to Him about my problems. I had hope beyond this life. This buoyed me up.

Yet in spite of my wonderful experience with God, I couldn't keep on top. I still resented the drudgery of my housework, hated being tied down constantly to numerous tasks and small children who needed my constant care, and felt that my husband didn't understand. Inside, a continuous battle raged.

Finally one day I saw my real problem: not my husband who could never quite understand what it was like to be tied down to babies twenty-four hours a day; not my noisy, demanding toddlers; but myself.

I realized that I had never really accepted my role as wife and mother. I expected my husband to fit into my concept of what a husband should be. Suddenly I saw that God wanted me to accept my husband as he was. I started thinking about his good points and realized that he had quite a few. He loved me and the children; he loved God as I now did; he was a hard worker and a good provider; he was patient with me.

I dropped to my knees again and asked God to change my attitude toward my husband. Right then and there I completely accepted the role God had given me as a wife and mother.

Almost immediately, things began to change.

I saw my job not merely as housekeeping but as homemaking. I pictured my task as a glorious profession. I really was a teacher, cook, interior decorator, seamstress, nurse, and many other things all in one.

With my change of attitude came an entirely new perspective. I threw myself into my job as a homemaker with all my heart. I stopped screaming at the children and tried to think of other ways to punish them than forever spanking. I learned to live the first part of 1 Peter 5:7, "Casting all your care upon him," taking comfort from the last part, "for he careth for you."

We are past the diaper and bottle stage now, but five children ages seven to sixteen keep a mother hopping. If I'm not taking my youngest son to boys' club, I'm settling a dispute, sewing a skirt for a clothes-conscious fifteen-year-old, or trying to explain to my sixteen-year-old why we don't do some things.

Sometimes I seem to meet myself coming and often drop off into bed at night exhausted as I did when the children were small. But the inner struggles and resentments are gone.

God has shown me that to be a homemaker and mother is one of the greatest tasks on earth. The day I accepted my job of wife and mother as a calling from the Lord, my chores turned into challenges. I wouldn't trade with anyone![1]

Causes of Resentments

Why was this young wife (I will call her Gloria) so resentful of the one she loved enough to marry? He did not fit into her idea of a husband. A woman tends to want to pack all the good qualities she has seen in other men into her own man!

Gloria's resentment also stemmed from a lack of preparation for her role as a homemaker—housekeeping routine, caring for a husband and children.

Housekeeping chores were not as glamorous as work in the hospital—in the public eye, surrounded by professional people, those she could converse with freely. At home she was very much alone.

1. "I Overcame My Resentment," *Power for Living*, Dec. 8, 1968. Copyright 1968, Scripture Press Publications, Inc., Wheaton, Ill. Reprinted by permission from Power for Living.

Right Step

But Gloria did what most of us do not want to do. She faced herself. In doing so, she realized she was a woman. She could not escape that! She had chosen marriage, a home, a family. Housekeeping comes along with this package!

Gloria took the right step. She admitted her resentment and focused on her husband's good qualities. Her feelings toward him changed completely.

These insights were good—and necessary. But they were not enough. She needed help outside of herself.

Trapped

I believe married women in today's radical feminist groups are Glorias who have not found Someone to help them. The feminist is running away from the real cause of her problems—herself. She is unwilling to accept herself as a woman equipped with female glands, organs, desires, and abilities. Unprepared for her role, she becomes tense, frustrated, irritated, resentful. She blames persons, and situations—cleaning, laundry, scrubbing, paying bills, changing diapers, running errands for husband—get her down. She begins to cry, "I'm trapped." From then on she claws at the trap, and spends her time planning how to get out of it.

Right Attitudes

Thank God, not every homemaker feels this way!

The basic difference is in a woman's attitude. She must substitute good thoughts for bad thoughts. The source of all good thoughts is God.

Someone has said when a woman feels that she is largely responsible for the kind of person her child will become, for her husband's well-being, and for making a good family life she receives and enjoys a satisfying, creative identity.

A former actress, Colleen Townsend, now a pastor's wife and mother of four children, relates how she overcame her resentments. One day she faced herself and simply told the Lord, "A career outside my home isn't what I want. But I'm desperate; I've got too much work to do. Show me how to have right attitudes."

The Lord did show her how to say no to demands and pressures from outside her home. He also showed her the need to keep in touch with Him daily so as not to lose her glow.

Gloria summed it up marvelously: "To be a homemaker and mother is one of the greatest tasks on earth. The day I accepted my job of wife and mother as a calling from the Lord, my chores turned into challenges. I wouldn't trade jobs with anyone."

Would you?

15

GET RID OF INNER TENSIONS

WHAT CAUSES inner tensions?

Some people think lots of work creates tensions.

That is what Roberta believes. She does her own housework, cares for two children, and frequently helps her husband with outside work. She is tense and nervous, fatigued and worn out. The doctor says that more rest and less tension would help. Instead, tension increases and rest is less.

You are sympathetic to Roberta. You think that with all that work, Roberta has just cause for her tensions.

WORK AND TENSION

However, doctors say that work in itself does not create tension any more than going sixty miles an hour gives one a headache. But forty miles per hour can bring on a headache if we are pushing ourselves to make the appointment and worrying that we will be late. The inner feeling is what matters. Worry as we travel, fear on the job, carrying inner grudges against our husband or children—all these result in tension headaches.

In Roberta's case, it was not the work, really. It was her attitudes and feelings which created her illness and inner tensions. She was afraid of the work in the months ahead and dreaded to see another day begin. She was discontented, and she resented the demands of a home and family.

LEARN TO RELAX

How can Roberta get rid of these inner tensions?

She should relax a few moments during the day with the children, take a leisurely stroll out-of-doors, or listen to soothing music, all the while focusing on the joys of her home, the blessings and rewards.

Dr. Jane W. McMullen reminds us that "if we want to get along in the modern age, we've got to learn how to shake off our tensions. In many parts of the world, the daily schedule allows for relaxation. In many countries it is customary to go home at noon, for lunch, and then stay home an added hour or two. In such cases, people have a chance to relax at a time of the day when relaxation is often very much needed. Such a habit makes it possible to do a better job with considerably less strain."[1]

TENSIONS ARE NORMAL

I personally think it would help Roberta to remind herself that some tensions are a part of life. She can expect them. Dr. George S. Stevenson, former president of the American Psychiatric Association, suggests that tensions can be our self-protective reactions to threats to our safety, our self-esteem, or our happiness.[2]

Tensions result from conflicts from living and working with other people. We all have different ways of thinking and acting.

They come from all areas of life—the job, community relationships, home, marriage relationships. Tensions

1. *Royal Neighbor*
2. "How to Deal with Your Tensions," *The Readers Digest*, March 1969, p. 89.

94

build when the children quarrel, when they make decisions differently than we had hoped, when everyone is in a hurry to get off in the morning and someone spills the milk.

Eva shares her solution in coping with these tensions: "I've found that a flash prayer helps me. When the milk is spilled, I think 'Oh, Lord, give me patience.' I pause for a split second. Then I can clean up the mess without blaming anyone."

HOW TO GET RID OF TENSION

Dr. George S. Stevenson suggests ways to rid yourself of tensions, in his article in *The Reader's Digest*, March 1969. In summary he says:

1. *Talk it out* with a confidant, with someone who will listen. Do not keep things bottled up.
2. *Escape for a while*, but then come back and deal with the problem in a composed way. How about escaping to a prayer closet or to the out-of-doors? Perhaps you can escape by listening to music, or by visiting a friend, or by doing something for someone else. But remember—come back, and face the problem.
3. *When anger makes you tense,* deal with it by doing physical work—cleaning out closets, mopping floors, or washing windows.
4. *Give in occasionally.* Yield to others, and behold, others then will begin yielding to you. This brings relief from tensions, plus a feeling of satisfaction. It helps resolve the problem. It is a step towards maturity. Had you thought of this one?
5. *Make out a list.* When work, or the thought of all the things you have to do, creates tension, schedule what has to be done. Pitch in and do the thing that has to be done first.

6. *Avoid the superwoman complex*—that you have to do everything, or that everything has to be perfect. Decide on what you can do, what your abilities are. Put your best into these. And do not take on too many outside responsibilities.

7. *Go easy with criticism.* Some women feel disappointed and frustrated when their husband or children do not measure up to expectations or fit into a preconceived pattern. We need to remember that each person is an individual, and has a right to develop as such. People who feel let down by shortcomings (real or imagined) of others are really let down about themselves. By finding out each one's good points and helping him to develop them, you become less critical.

8. *Give the other fellow a break.* Tense people often feel that they have to be there first. It may be in such an insignificant goal as getting ahead on the highway. Giving the other fellows a break can make things easier for yourself.

9. *Make yourself available.* Are you tense because you feel left out, slighted, or neglected? Often you just imagine this. Instead of shrinking away or remaining isolated, make the first move toward friendliness, or offer your help. It is healthier—and more practical.

10. *Include recreation in your day's schedule.* Every one of us ought to have a hobby into which we can throw ourselves completely, which we enjoy as we forget all about our work. Such a hobby might be raising flowers or house plants, playing a musical instrument, sewing, painting, or some activity or service outside the home.

11. *You need faith*—faith in yourself, faith in others, faith in moral values, and faith in God.[3]

3. Ibid., pp. 90-91.

96

We were missionaries living is an isolated area of Argentina. I enjoyed the work. It was God's choice for us. However, I did not appreciate all the details—isolation, new and difficult situations, the care and demands of four small children, never-ending daily chores, problems relating to the mission work, illness, and my husband absent much of the time.

I realize now that as much as anything, I resented his being away. I was fearful. I was discontent. I was lonely. I felt neglected. I was physically weak. I was full of self-pity. All of this was bottled up, tight.

Then it happened—probably just what you are thinking. I snapped.

And looking back, from an altogether different perspective, I can honestly say it was not the endless work—for I had always worked hard. It was not the new difficult situations—for I enjoyed adventure. It was not the aloneness—for I appreciated solitude at times.

It was not these.

It *was* my attitudes and feelings I brought into each day's situations.

How I wish I had known this—then.

Oh, yes, I often prayed. I believed God meets our needs. I prayed that God would iron out all the problems. I prayed that He would straighten out other people—make the children good, so they would quarrel less, keep my husband at home, we needed him. I asked that other people would be easier to get along with.

ASKED AMISS

I was asking amiss. As the Bible very plainly states: "You don't get answers to your prayers, because you're asking wrongly, asking for things I can't change." A normal child has a mind of his own—the basis of quarrels and conflicts. A man has to achieve at his job, even though it brings periods of absence. Tensions are a normal part of life.

Not aware of my actual needs, I had been wrongly asking God to remove tensions! What I should have been asking was for Him to change my attitudes, my feelings, in these normal situations.

But because He is God, He held on to me. He showed me what I did not know. He kindly taught me. I am still learning, to be sure, and sometimes fall short. I do know that lots of work, family relationships, new situations, disappointments, or tragedies do not *have* to get me down.

GOD'S PEACE

What is making you tense and nervous?

Talk it out with someone. Include God. Ask for right attitudes and feelings of joy, contentment, gratefulness, self-control, acceptance, understanding, gentleness, goodness, forgiveness, love, faith. He will give all of these and much more besides!

When you bring yourself, your reactions, your feelings, to Him, He will help you find a positive approach to each situation. He will help you keep everything in proper focus, help you find time for recreation, time to relax in the midst of all your duties and problems. He will help you get rid of inner tensions.

I know; He has done it for me.

16

LIVE SIMPLY

"THE TWENTIETH CENTURY MAN is miserable in the
midst of the miracles he has wrought. He is oppressed
by his own accomplishments and in fear of his own
inventions."[1]

Wordsworth wrote: "The world is too much with us;
late and soon, getting and spending, we lay waste our
powers."

And many of us wish we could get away from modern
complex living. Oh, for a simple life!

This was Thoreau's concern in the middle nineteenth
century: "Our life is frittered away by detail . . . simplify, simplify."

A SIMPLE LIFE

Simple living is life that is not complex—a life minus
the anxieties, the tensions, the frustrations of today's rat
race. It is a way of life without the clutter of excess
gadgets, easy wealth, and abundant knowledge which
lacks wisdom. It is a way of life that is honest, humble,
and sincere—not pretentious or superficial. A tranquil
life—with time to apply wisdom, love, concern, and
compassion.

Simple living indicates *contentment* with the basics of
life—food, clothing, and shelter. It includes *joy* in the

1. Eric Johnston, *Kiwanis* Magazine,

small things—a bird's song, new-fallen snow, clean windows, a child's smile and hug, the fireside. A simple life has *time* for an unhurried evening of family games and singing or reading together, family *prayers and Bible reading*—and a loyalty to God. It is a life of simple *faith* and lots of common sense.

Simple living can be the source of much happiness.

RICH WITH LITTLE

As far back as the sixteenth century, Edward Dyer wrote:

> Content I live; this is my stay,—
>   I seek no more than may suffice.
>
> These get with toile, and keepe with feare;
> Such cares my mind could never beare.
>
> Some have too much, yet still they crave;
>   I little have, yet seek no more.
> They are but poore, though much they have,
>   And I am rich with little store.
> They poor, I rich; they beg, I give;
> They lacke, I lend; they pine, I live.
>
> My wealth is health and perfect ease;
>   My conscience clere my chiefe defence.[2]

PEOPLE FORGOTTEN

What creates complex living? We are focusing on things, on great, impersonal achievements, rather than on the person—on man with an eternal soul.

Edwin Markham's poem reads:

Man-Making

> We are all blind, until we see
>   That in the human plan
> Nothing is worth the making if
>   It does not make the man.

2. Selections from "My Minde to Me a Kingdom Is."

Why build these cities glorious
If man unbuilded goes?
In vain we build the work, unless
The builder also grows.[3]

Compassion, concern, joy, gentleness, kindness, love, and humility build man. These are not acquired through the hustle and bustle of modern life and mere accumulation of facts. The characteristics that help people grow are passed on from person to person, from generation to generation, largely in the home.

POSSIBLE TO CHANGE?

However, simple living is possible. The other day, teenage Debbie remarked to her mother that she is glad they do not have lots of money. Their imagination and creativity have developed since they cannot go out and buy everything they want.

The father gave up a high-salaried position, and they moved to the country. They have learned to identify wild flowers and trees on their family strolls. They have simplified their eating and have exchanged complicated, expensive dishes for simple, wholesome food. They are healthier and happier too, reports Debbie's mother.

GOOD-BYE TO THE JONESES

Another family said good-bye to the "Joneses" and stopped trying to conform to the way of society.

The parents decided to live more simply one night after they discovered their fifteen-year-old son, Rick, drunk. They had purchased the liquor for a party. Horrified, they questioned him. He confessed he did not like it but wanted to keep up with his buddies. Telling of the changes that have since taken place, the mother reports:

3. Reprinted by permission of Kathleen Markham.

We're busy with a way of our own, a way that's much better for our family. It's a way that affords a new closeness in family relationships through time to understand and enjoy one another; it's a way that relieves tension—we're no longer living beyond our income; and it's a way that's leading us to real friendships and fulfillment in service to our church. We've given up the activities we didn't have time for, the clubs we couldn't afford, the frequent and large-scale entertaining; our clothes and our car will be old models before we replace them! And we're finding the freedom of being ourselves far more satisfying than following the Joneses' way of living.

It hasn't been easy to turn aside from one way of living and stick to another. But we're convinced that a change was necessary for family happiness and fulfillment. Now is an important time for our family; now David and I influence our children by our own way of living; now we need to give our children understanding and love and guidance to ease the roughness of adolescence and the teen years; now is the time to enjoy them and to give them an opportunity to enjoy us and their home.

A few months ago David gave up his extra job. We'll not be able to get a new stereo hi-fi set, nor have a professional decorator do our living room. But Rick and his father had an interesting time last night contriving their own stereophonic sound system from our old television set and a radio. And doing over the living room will be a family project.

Often during the past two years David and I have felt that we were losing touch with our children. There was little time for talk with them, especially from a casual approach. Now we have found that there are special times when the children want to talk, and do so freely if a parent is at home and is a relaxed and interested listener. For Karen this time is when she comes in after school, over a snack of apples, cookies, and milk.

Sue chats while we're in the kitchen preparing dinner or afterward as we wash dishes together. How swiftly that dishwashing time passes as I hear life from a teenager's viewpoint! (And I was losing all this in those busy days when I'd hurry dinner in order to get to a club meeting or party.)

Ricky is usually in a relaxed and talkative mood after his evening homework is done and seems then especially to enjoy his father's company. (How much more needful is this companionship than were the things that David's extra job earned for us!)

Further opportunity for family companionship and understanding is gained through our pleasant, recently acquired habit of having an evening snack of ice cream or popcorn—and talk!

We have time and energy now to do things with our children—a family skating party, a trip to our city's new museum of natural history. (The latter resulted in Karen's lively interest in fossil rocks—and a new hobby was begun.)

As we increase our activity in our church, we're making new friends with whom we have many interests in common. And we seem all to be on one level, regardless of the kind of clothes we wear, the model of car we drive, or the neighborhood that we live in.

Each week (on one of the afternoons I'd once have spent playing bridge) I've been visiting older persons who cannot leave their homes, an activity sponsored by our church women's society. And far more rewarding than the glamour of the social whirl is the welcome that these house-bound folk offer.

Our family is tithing now. So many things that we considered necessities when we were trying to keep up with the Joneses just don't seem a bit necessary any more.[4]

4. Source unknown.

This family's experience shows that it is possible to live simply, even in today's complex society, when we place true values of life first.

God sent us into the world with very few wants. Food, drink, clothing, and shelter are the basic physical necessities of life. With these met, I believe God intended that we'd spend time sharing and caring for each other, worshiping Him, enjoying nature, meditating on the good things of life.

But the more we have, the more we want. We have created many of our own problems. In our greed for more, in our reach for prestige, we have complicated life. We have brought upon ourselves tension, frustrations, disease, and illness.

GOD'S WAY

We have lost sight of true values. We have lost, too often, just plain common sense and temperate living. We have lost God.

"Why do you spend money for what is not bread, and your wages for what does not satisfy?" God asks. Then He continues, "Listen carefully to Me, and eat what is good, nourishes, and delight yourself in abundance . . . come to Me. Listen, that you may live" (Isaiah 55:2-3, NASB).

Enjoy life. Live simply—with God.

17

MOTHERS DO MAKE MISTAKES

YOU ARE on the road to positive living, to a good day when you are willing to admit you are not perfect!

When once you throw off that perfection mask and join the gang of homemakers, you will begin a new life—so will your family.

A friend of mine, Elizabeth Strachan, a former missionary wife and mother of several children, wrote the following article. With permission of the publishers, I am sharing the article with you.

> Let's be honest about it, mothers. We do make mistakes—many mistakes—and some of them tragic.
>
> For the sake of those women, most of whose lives are yet before them, I would like to point out a half dozen ways in which a young mother may fail her children, to her lifelong regret.
>
> 1. *Choosing the Wrong Daddy.* A mother isn't responsible for her own forbears, but she is responsible for choosing her children's father. Nothing she will ever do for her children is quite so important.
>
> One of the saddest conversations I ever had was with a young schoolteacher who had married a good-looking, charming man-about-town in no way suitable to be a father. Though the man caused his wife no end of heartaches, the one that overshadowed all

others was his influence on their children. Only those who seek divine guidance in courtship and marriage can avoid this almost irrevocable mistake.

2. *Beginning Too Late.* A noted authority on child-rearing once said that the answer to almost every problem connected with children is to begin a bit earlier.

One young mother came up to a speaker and asked him how soon she should begin the spiritual training of her child.

"How old is the child now?" he asked.

"Five."

"Oh, lady," the speaker answered in evident distress, "go home with haste. You have already lost the five best years."

I don't mean that you should push your children ahead of themselves or expect more of them than their age demands. Nevertheless, in nearly every field you will find that the earlier you begin, even on a simplified scale, to cultivate the virtues and qualities you want them to possess, the easier will be the task.

3. *Thinking that the Body Is More Important than the Soul.* The story is told of a young girl who received a gorgeous three-carat diamond ring from her fiance. The ring came in a beautiful little box. The foolish girl was so delighted with the little box that she scarcely noticed the diamond within.

Thousands of well-meaning mothers are making the same mistake. God sends them a treasure that is wrapped in a darling little body, and instead of giving their attention to the treasure within, they give it to their baby's box.

Your child's health and clothes are important, of course, but that isn't the part that will live forever! The invisible soul within is the true treasure, and it is only as you prepare that treasure for Christ have you fulfilled your task as a parent.

4. *Thinking Our Children Will Grow Up to Do What We Say, Rather than Copy What They See Us*

106

Do. Being a mother would be much simpler if this were true, but it is not.

We are told that 95 percent of what a young mother does with her child is in imitation of her own mother. Sometimes it seems as though our children would say to us, "What you do speaks so loudly, Mother, I can't hear what you say." And it is true of mothers, just as it is true of preachers, that "An ounce of walk is worth a pound of talk."

A mother can give scores of lectures on truthfulness, but her lectures will be more than worthless if her children hear her lie about their ages when buying a railway ticket. Perhaps the richest inheritance that a child can have is the memory of a holy mother.

5. *Failure to Pray*. The Bible and experience teach that what Tennyson said is true, "More things are wrought by prayer than this world dreams of." Prayer for our children before and after birth can bring more blessing to them than we can ever imagine. "He is able to do exceedingly abundantly above all that we ask or think" is what God offers to do for those who will bring their children to Him in prayer.

Prayer prepares our children for an early conversion, inclines their hearts toward the things of God, and gives them that blessing of God which "maketh rich." Mothers are very busy people. But if you are too busy to pray, mother, as someone has said, "you are too busy."

6. *Thinking Anything Else Is More Important than the Training of One's Children*. The world justly condemns the social butterfly mother, who neglects her children for parties and a good time. But children can also be neglected by mothers absorbed in good things: parent-teacher's activities, Christian work, and the affairs of the church.

Possibly no mother is so tempted to neglect her children as the missionary mother who is surrounded by so much need and opportunity. One of the saddest things I have ever read in missionary biography was

David Livingstone's admission that one of his chief regrets was that he neglected his own children.

Whatever our needs and weaknesses may have been or may be, we can bring them to God, and His grace is able to cover and overrule. We can pray in the words of the one who wrote:

> Dear Lord, take up my tangled strands,
> Where we have wrought in vain,
> That by the skill of Thy dear hands
> Some beauty may remain.
> Transformed by grace divine,
> Thy glory shall be Thine.

Nevertheless, the classic verse on this problem is found in Paul's letter to Timothy to the effect that he that does not care for his own is worse than an infidel and has denied the faith. (I Timothy 5:8).

For the average mother, this "sacrifice" means only about twenty years out of her seventy years of life. Most mothers then have around thirty years of service that they can give to the Lord and His work after their children go off to college. And those thirty years will not only be happier, but more fruitful, if she has been willing to let her children "tie her feet" as the Indian proverb puts it, when they were young.[1]

Each one of us must admit failure somewhere along the way.

But it is not too late to begin correcting errors. Let us begin right today, shall we?

I was thinking that only one of those mistakes is without remedy—that of choosing the wrong father for our children. However, on second thought, that is not either! God is able to overrule our mistakes. He can bring forth good from evil, if we want Him to.

Should you have failed in any areas of these six mistakes, the logical step now is to confess your error before

1. "Mothers Do Make Mistakes," *Moody Monthly,* May 1958. Used by permission.

God—beg His forgiveness. You can have the peaceful assurance that through His Son, Jesus Christ, He forgives. What is more, He *forgets* all about your error.

The second step is to really and truly *want* to do better. And just hand over to God your whole self—mind and thoughts, will, hands, feet, eyes, tongue! Let Him take over the controls from now on, as well as take care of the past! If any woman is in Christ Jesus, she is a new creature. Old things have passed away, behold, *all things* are become new!

What a powerful God we have!

18

I LOST MY FREEDOM

RECENTLY I was asked what was my greatest frustration with my job. I quickly mentioned, "Losing my freedom."

I am no longer free to pursue *as much as I would like to*—that creativity within me which cries for fulfillment as housekeeper, wife, mother, neighbor, and as a person.

Crown Princess Margreth of Denmark once remarked, "I'm not a person who has no other purpose in life than to clean house. However, I'm the kind of person who is extremely happy to be married and to have a house to clean."

I voice her feelings.

CREATIVE HOUSEWORK

I enjoy keeping house and doing the work that is necessary daily or occasionally. This includes cooking three meals a day, cleaning up the counters, washing the dishes, doing the laundry, putting away clean clothes, ironing (hopefully, before the time to wear the clothes), cleaning, and waxing floors.

These and the dozens of other household tasks belong in my schedule.

But since I took on my job, I no longer am free to do creative and leisurely cooking—to try out new recipes that do not come out of ready-made packages, to freeze and can fruits and vegetables. Most of the cooking is sandwiched between several other pressing duties.

I have resorted to drying most of the clothes indoors, no longer enjoying the fragrance of sun-dried, wind-blown clothes.

I lost my freedom to sew clothing to surprise the children and grandchildren.

I am not as creative in my housework as I wish to be. Time allows for necessary jobs done in a minimum amount of time.

However, I enjoy what I can do. Studies have shown that homemakers who feel housework is drudgery and a thankless job will find the work exhausting. On the other hand, women who view homemaking as a labor of love for the family find satisfaction and a feeling of creativity from providing for the family's needs.

HOBBIES

Since I work outside my home, I lost my freedom to creatively and leisurely enjoy my hobbies.

They are simple. They are little things. But they bring me pleasure and satisfaction—a well-kept lawn, flowering plants inside and outside the house. I used to have many. But they required special care. Now I have to be satisfied with rubber plants, cactus, and a few common, hardy plants that thrive even when neglected.

Another hobby is writing letters and freelance writing. Those, too, are limited.

SERVICE

Another area is service.

Love is serving, first at home, and then others beyond our cozy circle. In our materialistic, affluent, impersonal age, many cry, "No one cares!" We need to show we care as we reach out and touch the stranger, the new-comer living next door, the young mother so unsure of herself, with hardly enough time and energy to meet the children's continual demands. We need to touch the neglected child down the street, the misunderstood teenager, the unwanted senior citizen.

We also need to serve many others through church and community agencies.

I am challenged by the heartcries, "No one cares!" On a personal level I do what fits into my schedule, but I have had to pass by many personal opportunities as well as involvement in organized church and community projects.

RIGHT ATTITUDES

The key to a woman's fulfillment lies within herself, not in circumstances, glamor, or career. The key is her attitude.

Regardless of what else she aspires to do, a married woman needs right attitudes toward herself, the homemaker, and toward her home and family responsibilities. She should give these priority.

An outside job does not bring fulfillment if she does not enjoy a measure of success in her goals as wife and mother.

A woman finds her identity in relation with others—beginning at home: "There is satisfying creative identity for the woman who feels that she is the one most responsible for shaping the kind of person her child is to become—the most responsible for the well-being of her husband; the most responsible for making her family life good."[1]

Gwen has caught this truth. She writes:

> I have a three-year-old boy and two boys two months old and have been married for four years. . . . When I married I made up my mind that I was going to give my children a better life to live, better

1. *Redbook,* March 1966.

than what I had. It started with making my home a Christian home. That's one thing Mother never gave me.

I work in my house all day and for my children, enjoying it all as I do it. This is my life which is happier than ever.

I'm proud to be what I am. Proud that I've lived up to the things I wanted for my family. Proud of my house, my children, and my husband because there is love and respect from them to me.

This is one gal that loves all that I do no matter how bad things may get. I'm proud to do my housework because it is for my family.

This is beautiful. A homemaker *available* to her family, leisurely doing and caring for husband and children.

A full-time housekeeper is her own boss from nine to five. She is free to arrange her day, to change her schedule if necessary, to enjoy sharing with and caring for the family all hours of the day.

I have relinquished all that. No longer can I, at the drop of a suggestion, accompany my husband to town, to visit a parishioner, to take off the afternoon and go to the mountain, to visit our families. No longer am I free during the day to enter into the children's play, hobbies, and work side-by-side, to share, to chat, to argue, to challenge them. Nor am I able to entertain their friends whenever they wish, nor to baby-sit for the grandchildren.

I am *bound* within certain hours. I am not always available whenever their needs arise—not available for a word of encouragement, a moment of listening, or a time of helping.

QUIET TIMES

I also need to be available for myself, to meet my needs for inner strength and power.

113

Ours is a noisy age. There are the "public noises"—jets, cars, air hammers, lawn mowers, all the sounds of an ever-increasing mechanical age. I cannot do much about these.

But there is another kind of noise I need to do something about *now*. It is the racket of everyday living—the sounds from the radio, TV, hollering at one another, the noisy crowd. It is the inner noise—fear, fantasies, and all kinds of distracting thoughts. This inner commotion needs to be silenced before I can achieve outer silence.

I have found it is possible to eliminate these inner noises in a few minutes, as I empty my mind of every thought, of everything but the presence of God.

The poet Samuel Hageman wrote, "to be alone with silence is to be alone with God."

I talk over the distractions with God, and leave them with Him. Then my mind is clean and clear for His thoughts and His ideas.

A homemaker can choose a few moments alone while making the beds, or in the laundry room, or over a cup of coffee after everyone leaves in the morning, or when the children are napping, or a few moments alone in nature.

Many years ago when our children were small, I wrote,

The Quiet Place

I like to find
A quiet place
Amidst the work
And pressing pace—
And shift my thoughts
To God— and grace.

Then struggles, cares
And fears release.
He speaks in love.
He gives me peace.

114

Fresh courage comes.
My tensions cease.

I love to find
This quiet place!

PERIODS OF SOLITUDE

When our youngest child was small, during her nap time I was free to spend several hours in Bible study and prayer, in meditation, in an evaluation of life, of society, of happenings.

During another period, I got up at 5:00 A.M. in order to fix a bite to eat before our boys took off on a paper route. After they left, I had those moments of meditation and prayer before beginning the day. I was free to nap later on.

Now, these daily periods of solitude and renewal are rare. I have to find the scarce moments of silence between deadlines, and between pressures of trying to meet the demands of both homemaking duties and a job.

However, I remind myself to get rid of the daily sound—to remember God's words: "Be still and know that I am God" (Psalm 46:10).

FULFILLMENT

Lest I leave you with the wrong impression, let me clarify. I am happy to have a house to clean. I find fulfillment in being a wife, mother, and housekepeer. I did not need an outside job to find fulfillment. God led me into where I am. And although I have lost freedom to find the fully satisfying creative identity of a *leisurely* housewife, God gives me many rewards. I try not to focus on what I have lost, but to pull out these rewards. I do find a joy in this creative ministry to homemakers.

115

19

EVERYONE NEEDS LOVE

LOVE IS AN AFFECTION which endears us to another.

Love recognizes each person as a human being, made in the image of God.

Love signifies "respect for the inner man, for his spirit," says Roy Wilkins. "Until we have that love, until it supplants greed and grasping and combativeness and abrasiveness, we're going to have trouble everywhere."

Love is an old-fashioned formula, but it is very up to date.

A poet wrote about love, made of tenderness, dreams, hopes, fantasies; however, he concludes, "But love that lasts a lifetime is of more material stuff," like patience in difficulties, understanding each other's goals, accepting each one's quirks, grinning at silly things we do in our daily relationships.

Dave Wilkerson, founder and director of *Teen Challenge,* says, "Love is not something you feel. It is something you do."

LOVE ACCEPTS EACH CHILD

The tragic generation gap could be bridged if parents loved their sons and daughters, regardless of age, and if sons and daughters loved their parents, regardless of differences of opinion and experiences.

116

Love accepts each child with his or her individual personality.

Two small boys in a class had the same last name but were very different in their appearance. The teacher asked them if they were brothers.

"Yes," replied the one, "but one of us is adopted, and I forgot which one." Love had erased the difference!

Many parents make the mistake of thinking that providing material things, proper nutrition, education, music, is showing love. This is only a small part of love!

Someone has said, "Comparable to the key nutrients in food are the key emotional nutrients contained in the love and security with which parents surround their children. No list or chart can possibly convey the life-sustaining force of Mother's tenderness, Father's smile, their fondling of the child, their reassuring words. Right from the start, the child experiences through the sense of touch the feeling of being loved and wanted, of being someone of worth in a world not to be feared."

There is no substitute for love and cuddling and a feeling of being wanted and appreciated. This is the child's security.

"The greatest terror a child can have is that he is not loved, and rejection is the hell he fears," says the famous child psychologist, Dr. Hiam Ginott.

LOVE AT HOME

Love identifies with the child's feelings.

Love learns to relate positively.

Love spends time with the child in his world of play and imagination.

Love listens.

Love does not force him daily into an adult mold.

Love keeps in touch at every age and stage.

Love sets limits for the good of the child.

Love disciplines and teaches responsibility.

Love forgives even when the ball accidentally breaks the car window.

Love lets the youth try some of his methods.

Love lets the teenage girl make salads and cakes as well as peel the potatoes, clean the floor, and wash dishes.

Authorities agree that the root of today's crime, delinquency, and drug problems is the parent's rejection of their children.

"I Love You, Johnny"

"I love you, Johnny," said Mother one day.
"I love you more than I can say."
Then she answered his questions with, "Don't bother me now;"
And just didn't have time to show him how
To tie his truck to his tractor and plow.
But she washed her windows and scrubbed the floor
And baked and cooked and cleaned some more.
"Bring the neighbor in? Well I should say not.
You'll track up my floors and I don't want a spot.
No, we won't have time for a story today.
Mother's cooking for company, so run out and play.
Maybe tomorrow," she said with a sigh,
And Johnny went out almost ready to cry.
"I love you, Johnny," again she said
As she washed his face and sent him to bed.
Now how do you think that Johnny guessed
Whether 'twas he or the house that she really loved best?[1]

MARY KLASSEN

MARITAL LOVE

Love in the home begins with a husband's and wife's love for each other, including physical love. Marital love is much more than physical love, although sex is included and important. Marital love is based on understanding, on compassion, on caring and sharing together.

1. Used by permission of *The Wesleyan Advocate*.

"Love," replies a well-known family counselor, "is the solution to family trouble." It begins between husband and wife. Children learn how love acts from them. This counselor hears many speak of the marriage and home as working on a 50-50 basis of authority. "However," he continues, "in all my counseling I have not yet discovered such a marriage. Life just doesn't work out that neatly. And where love is more prevalent we hear much less about the 50-50 idea."[2]

The Bible recognizes woman's perfect spiritual equality with man. On the other hand, it recognizes and secures man's responsible leadership. Every home—like every society, school, corporation, state, or nation—must have a recognized head. Within the normal family, God has ordained that man take this leadership.

"LOVE YOUR WIFE"

The Bible says, "Husbands, love your wives, even as Christ also loved the church, and gave himself for it" (see Ephesians 5:25).

That leaves no room for a man to be a dictator, a bully, or a fanatic. Such love is understanding and compassionate.

In his book, *The Essence of Marriage,* Dr. Julius H. Fritz, a clinical marriage counselor of Dallas, Texas, says that man should take the initiative to provide this love. The emotional relationship between a male and a female is called marriage. Since love is this emotion, the responsibility for success or failure of marriage is basically the man's. "This is the design of creation."

Dr. Fritz is convinced that to be successful and fulfilled, a wife depends greatly on the atmosphere of love with which her husband surrounds her. To envelop her with emotional security—love, tenderness, considera-

2. Rev. A. Purnell Bailey, from a General Features Corp. article. © 1957.

tion, kindness, benevolence, cordiality, acceptance, she will go where he wants to take her, and do what he must do. It will not be difficult for her to submit to him and be supportive.

If lacking his love, if unable to depend on her husband for emotional security, she becomes anxious. This rejection creates deep emotional problems. Dr. Fritz explains that being a helpmate to her husband—her purpose from creation—is hindered, and "she is denied her innate need in order to fulfill this purpose—being loved."[3]

MAN NEEDS LOVE

In turn, a man also needs love, acceptance, courtesy, consideration, and understanding. A woman's love, respect, and devotion make him want to love her. To compete with, to nag, or to dominate him drives him away. He then builds wall of resistance and isolation.

Love listens. Love tries to understand and identify with his needs and interests. Love makes him feel he is the greatest. Love focuses on his good qualities, not his faults.

A woman's love can help a man want to change his life.

Anita and her husband had grown apart. One day she admitted her lack of love and asked God to help her save their marriage. She began to be sensitive to her husband's wishes. She prepared his favorite foods. She developed an interest in his outdoor life. She helped him whenever she could in the shop. She wrote little love notes and included them in his lunch, all the while praying for God's love to reach him. And it did, after several years.

Eugenia Price says we have to allow love to become

3. *The Essence of Marriage* (Grand Rapids: Zondervan, 1971).

a habit. We do this by practicing all we can see of it in our day-by-day relationships. She explains, "It is a gift, but we must form the habit of using the gift or it lies worthless in the drawer of our inertia."[4]

EVERYONE NEEDS LOVE

Love must be expressed, both in words and in practical deeds. The person who sees someone with a need and passes the other way, "How can the love of God dwell in him?"

Love includes your enemy. Love returns evil with good.

Some years ago a farmer friend was losing grain from his bin. So he hid himself in his granary for several nights. One night a man entered, snapped on the light, and started filling his sack. The farmer stepped out of the shadow, helped him fill his sack, and carried it to his car! Needless to say, he lost no more grain!

Thousands of lives are wasting away in our state hospitals, not because they are mental cases, but because no one loves them.

Wars, racial tension, strife, fanatical revolutionary groups, crime, drugs, delinquency, immorality, all point to one cause—lack of love.

THE SECOND MILE

Stern Duty said, "Go walk a mile
    And help your brother bear his load."
I walked reluctant, but, meanwhile
    My heart grew soft with help bestowed.
Then Love said, "Go another mile."
    I went, and Duty spoke no more,
But Love arose and with a smile
    Took all the burden that I bore.
It's ever thus when Duty calls;
    If we spring quickly to obey,

4. *Make Love Your Aim* (Grand Rapids: Zondervan, 1967), preface.

Love comes, and whatever befalls,
 We're glad to help another day.
The second mile we walk with joy;
 Heaven's peace goes with us on the road,
So let us all our powers employ
 To help our brother bear life's load.

STEPHEN MOORE

Goethe wrote, "We are shaped and fashioned by what we love."

Love is a gift of God. "God is love." When we love Him, we love others, because God loves them.

Love never ends.

20

A KITCHEN SAINT

ARE YOU a kitchen saint?

Is it possible to keep calm, content, and joyful?

Can a homemaker face her daily chores and reverses in the kitchen and home with poise and a cheerful spirit?

Our own efforts can accomplish this for a short time, perhaps an hour or so, but not all day long—from the time the baby's cries awaken us at 5:00 A.M. till the last one is tucked in at night!

A homemaker largely determines the general atmosphere in the home—whether it is tense, full of hostility and bitter feelings, or warm, loving, helpful, and cooperative.

She needs a song on her lips and a song in her soul, "though the waves of distress around her should roll!"

It's easy to wear a pleasant disposition and to speak kindly when the children are not quarreling or our work goes according to schedule. Under such circumstances it takes no effort at all to be pleasant.

Someone has said that to keep calm and cheerful when everything goes wrong, is the best way to show to others that we belong to God and that a power beyond ourselves controls us.

And that is so right! Jesus once told His followers that to love those who love us is no test of His love in our hearts. To love a thoughtless, unkind husband, to love a disobedient child, to love the quarreling children—these prove His love in our hearts.

God's presence—His power and love—enables us housewives to face our daily routine and responsibilities with joy and peace.

He gives us a change of mind—new attitudes, new thoughts, new goals, and new motives. He lifts us from self, from the mundane to see the importance of the task.

He gives us a new vision of who we are and who we can be.

He gives us a desire to be better homemakers—to be kinder, gentler, more understanding, more appreciative, more loving, and more unselfish.

When we are tempted to think only of the mending, the scrubbing, the stubbed toes, the formulas, the fussings, and such, we need to fill our minds immediately with thoughts of thanksgiving.

We need to follow this advice from the Bible, "Whatever is true, whatever is honorable, whatever is right, whatever is pure, whatever is lovely, whatever is of good repute, if there is any excellence and if anything worthy of praise, let your mind dwell on these things" (Philippians 4:8, NASB).

We can repeat (over and over again, if necessary) these statements, "I'm engaged in the most wonderful career in the world! I love my husband and children. I'm grateful for their love and companionship, for their kindness, for a home. God has placed me here and I'll do my best. God created me a woman with the unique equipment to be a helper to my husband, to love and nurture our children. I would not trade this career for any other. After all, the dazzle of outside careers is only a veneer—underneath is cheap wood."

Helen Keller says, "Woman's sphere is the home, and

the home, too, is the sphere of man. The home embraces everything we strive for in this world. To get and maintain a decent home is the object of all our best endeavors."

COUNT YOUR BLESSINGS

Take time, often, to just sit down and enumerate all the reasons why you are thankful. Compare yourself with any one of your acquaintances who does not have a husband, or who does not have children or a home of her own. Or think of the many women and children without husbands and fathers, without homes, in war-torn areas. Absolutely nothing else in this world can bring the inner satisfaction, contentment, and peace which human love and fellowship in a family environment bring to the human heart.

"The domestic affections are the principal source of human happiness and well-being" (Charles W. Eliot).

OUR MISSION FIELD

To enjoy fully this happiness and contentment means cutting ourselves off from some legitimate activities. Because they have their hands tied at home, some housewives think they are not doing anything for their Lord. They sigh, "If only I'd be a missionary, or have a prominent part on some committee, or be a youth leader, or something similar, then I *could* do something worthwhile."

One time after D. L. Moody preached a challenging missionary sermon, a lady came to him. She asked if he could find a place for her on the mission field. She did so much want to serve the Lord.

Upon questioning her, Mr. Moody soon discovered she had six children. He immediately exclaimed, "Lady, your mission field is right at home!"

That is right, mothers, we are responsible for those immortal souls God has loaned to us. We are the sculptors and they are the living statues. We shape the eternal destiny of their souls. Ours is a *divinely* appointed task.

A happy Christian home is a tiny circle of heaven on earth. In it our children learn of God's eternal truths and values; they learn of His claims on their lives. Human love and joys give a faint glimpse of heavenly thrills awaiting the one who loves God.

ONE DISILLUSIONED MOTHER

Several years ago I met a young mother who was practically ruining her own life and that of her husband and two little children. She was a nervous wreck and needed psychiatric help.

As a young girl, she had offered her life to God as a missionary nurse to Africa. She became a trained nurse. But somewhere along the way, she fell in love with a young man and married him. When reverses and babies came in quick succession, Satan had her think she should not have married. She should have gone to Africa. Consequently the children annoyed her. Her husband's occupation displeased her. Her house became a prison.

My heart ached for this mother. She did not know that her mission field was right with her. She was not aware of the challenge which was hers to create a godly atmosphere in her home by which she could bring God to her family. She could only think of greener pastures on the other side of the fence.

MARY'S APPROACH

Contrast this with another mother, whom we will call Mary. Included in her circle of close friends were homemakers actively engaged in religious activities. Mary felt left out, she longed to do something special for God, but—she was only a housewife.

126

Well, to make a long story short, she led all her family to know God through Jesus. Her children's friends preferred her hospitality above others. On moving day, new neighbors found in her a warm friend, as she brought over her favorite pie. The crippled, the shut-ins, and the sick in the community enjoyed her tasty food. And one night, as the prayer group met for regular fellowship, Mary and her husband brought a new couple along— one that had only recently found the Lord through Mary's influence!

YOU CAN BE A KITCHEN SAINT

I would say Mary was a kitchen saint.

I will go a bit further. All of us can be Marys. Too often we are Marthas—bogged down with serving and with the routine chores. We have a "Mary mind but Martha hands."

I believe that somewhere along the daily path it is possible to blend these two into a kitchen saint!

The story is related that my husband's grandmother used to kneel beside each child's bed as she made it in the morning, and prayed for the child by name. Is it any wonder that her eleven children were lovers of God and that several became ministers?

Grandmother Miller's influence reaches down even today to the third and fourth generation of Christian workers, missionaries, and parents.

Friend, let us accept the divine challenge of our career.

As we see the loaf of bread, let us pray that our family will receive heavenly bread to nourish their souls.

As we wash their clothes, let us pray that their filthy rags of self-goodness will be washed white in the blood of Calvary.

As we polish shoes, let us pray that their feet may ever walk in the right road.

127

As we wash dirty faces and hands, let us pray they might be kept from sin and evil.

As we hear of needy ones in our community and the world, let us lend a helping hand, "as unto the Lord."

Daily let us remember what the Bible says, "Whatever you do, do your work heartily (cheerfully) as for the Lord rather than for men; knowing that from the Lord you will receive the reward of the inheritance. It is the Lord Christ whom you serve" (Colossians 3:23-24, NASB).

Will you be a kitchen saint and let God have a hand in everything you do?

Moody Press, a ministry of the Moody Bible Institute, is designed for education, evangelization and edification. If we may assist you in knowing more about Christ and the Christian life, please write us without obligation to: Moody Press, c/o MLM, Chicago, Illinois 60610.